THE EASY MEAT COOKBOOK

The *The* EASY
MEAT COOKBOOK

75 Simple Recipes for Beef, Pork, Lamb, Veal, and Poultry

JENNIFER OLVERA

Photography by Andrew Purcell

ROCKRIDGE
PRESS

Cover Designer: Jay Dea
Interior Designer: Joshua Moore
Art Producer: Megan Baggott
Editor: Marjorie DeWitt
Production Editor: Emily Sheehan
Photography © 2020 Andrew Purcell. Food styling by Carrie Purcell.
Author photo courtesy of Michael Runez

ISBN: Print 978-1-64739-811-8 | eBook 978-1-64739-486-8
R0

To Aunt Greta, who taught me to find beauty, joy, and wonder everywhere—especially in what's easily overlooked

CONTENTS

Introduction xi

1

THE FUNDAMENTALS OF COOKING MEAT 1

2

 BEEF 17

3

 PORK 59

4

LAMB AND VEAL 101

 POULTRY 125

INTRODUCTION

Many of my fondest childhood memories revolve around food. I was the little kid writing a recipe for stuffed mushrooms, reveling in a backyard pig roast, and surveying the potluck dishes at my parents' boat club gatherings. My first self-cooked dinner? Cheeseburger soup, as a kindergartener. Too short to reach the stove unaided, I stirred it while standing on a kitchen chair.

As time passed, my interest only grew. After graduating from DePaul University, I worked as a journalist, first at community newspapers, then as a freelance food and culinary travel writer for publications like the *Chicago Tribune*, the *Chicago Sun-Times*, and the *Los Angeles Times*. Expanding my repertoire, I served as a dining critic for *Chicago* magazine. For me, however, it wasn't enough to simply *write* about food. I wanted in on the action. A former columnist for *Serious Eats*, I'm now fortunate to be publishing my seventh book and my fourth cookbook.

As I began testing and developing recipes and traveling internationally, I was on a quest to discover local fare I could recreate at home. During that time, something became apparent: I view the world through a culinary lens. It's no wonder. Pretty much everything—history, culture, the economy, traditions, one's sense of community and family—is inextricably linked to food.

Cooking is about more than sustenance to me. Food transforms and informs your worldview, widens your horizons, and whisks you to balmy climes when the weather is cold and gray. Beyond filling your home with comforting scents, home-cooked meals nurture, sustain, and unite those who gather together to "break bread."

It's in that spirit I share this book and my deep-seated love of meat. Trust me, I love a well-crafted vegetable dish—I really do. But this girl can't live on fruit and veggies alone. Included in this book are some dear favorites, such as the roast chicken I have made for my sons from the time they were young, as well as a family recipe for chicken adobo, lovingly taught to me by my partner's mom. In these pages, you'll find 75 easy recipes that will help you make great, protein-centric meals out of grocery store cuts without a bunch of specialized equipment. Let's get cooking!

The Fundamentals of COOKING MEAT

Properly prepared meat is a glorious thing. To get the most out of your cuts, there are a few overarching principles. You use high heat to brown meat and develop flavor (a process called the Maillard reaction, named for the French chemist who first described it in the early 1900s). Slow-and-low cooking preserves moisture and prevents overcooking. Tender cuts lend themselves to quick cooking styles, while tougher ones generally need more time. It's also important to remember that heat rises as meat rests. As such, you should remove it from heat 5° to 10°F below your desired serving temperature. Last, but not least, always let your meat rest before cutting and serving it to allow the juices to redistribute. A thin steak or chop should rest for 5 to 10 minutes; a thicker roast for 15 to 20 minutes; and a large roast, such as a turkey, can rest for about 40 minutes before being carved.

HOW TO SHOP

As a young girl, I remember going to the local butcher, its jovial staff a font of protein knowledge. Each time felt like a special occasion—the meat lined up just so, some with house marinades. Although I have since moved away, I make an annual holiday pilgrimage to the same meat market for a thick, beefy prime filet mignon. Why? Because a local butcher is a place of great worth.

Still, I know not everyone has the time or resolve to make that extra stop. Rest assured, a well-stocked grocery store with a good meat counter will certainly do. Prefer the wholesale chains? Costco brims with quality cuts. You won't find the same wealth of options as you will at an independent market, but depending on what you're cooking, that may be just fine.

No matter where you shop, make the most of your experience by talking to a butcher. Ask questions, glean tips, and make sure you know what the appropriate cooking temps, times, and techniques are. Not sure *what* to ask? Start here.

Q: What's fresh?
A lot of markets and butchers process meat in house, so they can easily tell you what's fresh. You might even be able to see the sausages being made in house.

Q: What do you recommend?
It's safe to say every butcher has a favorite less-expensive, less-common cut of meat. Don't be afraid to inquire.

Q: What cut of meat would you recommend for the dish I am making?
When in doubt, ask your butcher what cut to use for, say, that cassoulet or Grilled Chimichurri Flank Steak (page 34). While you're at it, get some advice on the best ways to bring out its best flavor and texture.

Q: What's the best cut for my budget?
While recipes sometimes list the most expensive option, your butcher can turn you on to similar or better options, sometimes for a song.

Q: What do you make in-house?
Whether it's grinding burgers, preparing sausage, marinating meat, or stuffing cuts, butchers have a few tricks up their sleeves. Be sure to take advantage.

Q: Where do you source your meat?

Knowing an animal was humanely raised locally matters. How and where an animal was raised affects the taste and texture of meat.

Q: How would you prepare, cook, slice, and serve this cut of meat?

The folks behind your local meat counter don't just sell meat; they're often meat evangelists, too. Ask a seasoned butcher how they prepare and serve a particular protein at home.

Q: Can you prepare an item for me?

From spatchcocking (splitting open to prepare for grilling) a chicken to trimming chops to custom-grinding meat with your preferred blend, butchers are more than happy to lend a hand.

COOKING EQUIPMENT

Unless you're in college cooking ramen and boxed mac and cheese, you likely see the merit of having a well-stocked kitchen, particularly when it comes to cooking meat and poultry. Having the right tools to get the job done opens up your culinary horizons and has everything to do with the quality of the dishes you turn out. These are essentials you should not be without.

Baking Dish

More flexible in size than a roasting pan, a baking dish (aka casserole dish) can be made out of glass, ceramic, or even cast iron, such as the ones from Le Creuset. Available in round, square, and oblong versions, either shallow or deep, the baking dish is meant for use in the oven. Be sure to have a 9-by-13-inch one on hand.

Baking Sheet

Also called a baking tray or sheet pan, a baking sheet is an indispensable flat, rectangular metal pan that's used in the oven to bake everything from bread to meat. It's a good idea to own both 9-by-13-inch and 18-by-13-inch sizes.

Common Package Labels

Have you ever wondered what the various meat designations mean? It's no wonder, since the terms are largely cloaked in mystery. Here's the lowdown.

CAGE-FREE

In this case, chickens can roam around without cages. However, they're still housed in a building with confined space, without access to the outdoors. In addition to not seeing sunshine or eating fresh grass, they're fed the same as conventional chickens.

CONVENTIONALLY RAISED

Conventionally raised meat and poultry comes from animals fed conventional food, such as grain treated with pesticides, herbicides, fungicides, and fertilizers. It's important to note that by-products end up being stored in the animals' bodies. Also, conventionally raised animals are kept in confined quarters day and night, without space to roam.

FREE-RANGE, PASTURE-RAISED, OR FREE-ROAMING

While not necessarily organic, free-range animals do not live in cages or confined spaces and are allowed access to the outside. However, there is no designation for their feed, which may include animal by-products, corn, grain, or soy. The terms "free-roaming" and "pasture-raised" are often used interchangeably. While these words conjure images of animals in nature, eating natural foods and basking in sunlight, no government regulations in the United States ensure this is true.

GRAIN-FED

Grain-fed—or "conventionally raised"—cows are moved to a feedlot once they're weaned from their mother's milk, usually around 8 months of age. Then the cows are fed grains, corn, and soy to fatten them up and increase farmers' yield.

GRASS-FED

Grass-fed usually refers to cattle that began by eating a grass diet but then received supplemental grain or transitioned to a completely grain-based diet.

GRASS-FINISHED

Once weaned from their mother's milk, grass-finished cattle chomp on nothing but grass, foraged food, and possibly, supplemental natural foods like alfalfa sprouts during winter, for the remainder of their lives.

ORGANIC

Organic meat, poultry, eggs, and dairy products come from animals that never received antibiotics or growth hormones. Organic food is produced without using most conventional pesticides, fertilizers made with synthetic ingredients or sewage sludge, bioengineering, or ionizing radiation. Additionally, an organic animal must have access to the outdoors and have enough space to move around, as defined by the USDA.

VEGETARIAN-FED

Vegetarian-fed refers to animals raised on a vegetarian diet without animal products. This label is usually applied to chickens. Do note that chickens are omnivores by nature.

You may find yourself wondering, "What do I choose?" I'd encourage you to buy the most naturally raised option your budget allows. Purchasing mindful meat is undoubtedly more expensive. However, it's also an investment in your health.

Boning Knife

Best for cutting and boning fish, meat, and poultry, a boning knife features a sharp point and narrow blade so it can move and flex to separate meat from the bone and slice through joints and cartilage. However, it should never be used to cut through bones. A boning knife, and a chef's knife, prove indispensable when prepping meat.

Butcher's Twine

Butcher's twine is used to truss (bind together the wings and legs) poultry, secure stuffed meat, tie roasts so they keep their shape, and tie handfuls of herbs. Additionally, it can be used to tie sausage and for curing, drying, and smoking meats.

Cast-Iron Skillet

Affordable, versatile, and oh-so-heavy, a cast-iron skillet holds heat and distributes it evenly. It does a great job of browning without scorching. Plus, it's nonstick when properly seasoned (see page 10). Beyond lasting a lifetime when properly cared for, a cast-iron skillet can be used on the stovetop and in the oven, for sautéing, searing, and baking alike. Look for a pan that's at least ⅛-inch thick and 10 to 12 inches in diameter.

Chef's Knife

The most important knife in your arsenal, a chef's knife is your go-to for almost every kitchen task. It can be 6 to 12 inches long and typically features a broad blade which tapers upward to a point, allowing the knife to rock backward and forward when mincing. One with a greater length, such as 10 inches, is ideal for faster, easier slicing. However, if you have small hands, a shorter 8-inch knife is easier to control. It should never be used to butcher or carve meat; only to slice, cube, or chop it.

Dutch Oven

Featuring a thick bottom and sides, a Dutch oven has a tight-fitting lid to trap moisture, distribute heat evenly, and maximize flavor. With the lid off, it can be used to brown meat and vegetables atop the stove. It can also be placed in the oven for braising. Find a heavy 5- or 6-quart Dutch oven with thick sides and a thick bottom. It should be oven-proof and, ideally, made of enameled cast iron.

Grill Pan

Used on top of the stove, a grill pan features ridges similar to grill grates. In addition to creating grill marks on food, these ridges let fat drain. You can use a grill pan to cook most anything you'd cook on the grill, including steak, chicken, fruit, and kebabs. Ideally, the pan is made of cast iron. When grilling for a crowd, opt for a large one that fits across two burners.

Kitchen Shears

Helpful when it comes to snipping herbs, cutting open food packaging, and breaking down poultry, heavy-duty, multipurpose kitchen shears are a must-have.

Meat Mallet

A meat mallet is used to tenderize meat, or soften its fibers, so it's easier to chew and digest. Use it when you're preparing particularly tough cuts.

Meat Thermometer

A meat thermometer is used to measure the internal temperature of meat. The best and most accurate are instant-read digital thermometers. A good-quality instant-read thermometer can provide an accurate reading within 3 or 4 seconds, allowing you to confidently serve meat cooked to a safe temperature. On the non-digital side? Look for a well-calibrated, oven-going meat thermometer that can remain in the meat while it's roasting in the oven or cooking on the grill. Whichever one you choose, it should be inserted at least 2 inches into the center of the largest muscle or into the thickest portion of the meat, away from bones.

Nonstick Skillet

Your kitchen is not complete without the ease of a good nonstick pan, preferably ceramic-coated. With slanted sides, it's perfect for panfrying breaded meat, as well as cooking seafood and eggs. As its name implies, ingredients won't stick to its surface. In order to preserve the coating of a nonstick pan, never use metal utensils or abrasive tools, and don't place the pan in the dishwasher. Simply soak and clean it with a soft cloth and dish soap.

Paring Knife

A paring knife looks like a smaller, simpler version of a chef's knife and features a short blade, usually between 2½ and 4 inches long. It's ideal for tasks that require attention to detail. This includes slicing and mincing garlic, peeling apples, and hulling strawberries.

Plastic Cutting Board

Plastic cutting boards are a kitchen essential because they're easy to sanitize, making them well-suited for raw meat preparation. On the downside, cutting on them tends to leave grooves where bacteria can hide. Clean them in hot, soapy water or in your dishwasher. To prevent bacteria growth, it's also a good idea to occasionally flood the surface with a solution of 1 gallon of water plus 1 tablespoon of bleach. Rinse them with plain water afterward; then, clean and fully dry them standing upright before storing.

Roasting Pan

Roasting pans are a necessity for cooking large meats, such as a whole turkey, a whole chicken, or a pork roast. Because their sides are relatively low, meat browns while retaining its yummy juices. A roasting pan's size allows you to cook meat and vegetables together. Once your dish is cooked, you can remove the meat and vegetables, transfer the pan to the stovetop, and make a pan sauce to finish your dish. Choose a heavy-bottomed roasting pan that fits your oven and features riveted, easy-to-grip handles. A 13-by-16-inch pan typically works well. Go with a model that isn't nonstick—it will produce the best sauces.

Saucepan

A classic 3- or 4-quart saucepan features tall, straight sides that prevent rapid moisture loss. This makes it a go-to for steaming, blanching, simmering soup, and, of course, making a sauce. Seek out a lidded saucepan with walls that are as thick as its bottom to promote even heat distribution.

Sauté Pan

A sauté pan has straight sides and a larger surface area, making it the perfect choice for searing meat, reducing a pan sauce, and panfrying, searing, and browning foods. It can hold a higher volume of liquid without taking up much oven space. When its lid fits tightly, a sauté pan also minimizes evaporation.

Stockpot

A real workhorse in the kitchen, an 8- to 10-quart stockpot can be used to cook large quantities of soup and broth, make a big batch of chili, or boil up to 2 pounds of pasta. Buy a heavy one with durable handles.

Wood Cutting Board

Wood tends to be harder to sanitize though it's tougher overall. As a result, you won't see as many deep scratches in the surface. Wash wood cutting boards by hand in hot, soapy water. Allow them to dry upright. Consider opting for harder materials, like bamboo and maple, and look for ones that feature a well along the perimeter to catch meat juices. For board maintenance, generously sprinkle coarse salt over the surface of the board every few weeks. Then, rub it with a sliced lemon and rinse well with hot water.

Cast-Iron Pan Seasoning and Care

Preparing and caring for a cast-iron skillet is easier than you think.

TO SEASON YOUR SKILLET

1. Scrub the skillet in hot, soapy water and dry thoroughly.

2. Spread a thin layer of melted shortening or vegetable oil all over the inside and outside of the skillet.

3. Place it upside down on the middle rack of an oven heated to 375°F, with foil beneath to catch any drips.

4. Bake for 1 hour, then let cool in the oven.

TO CLEAN YOUR SKILLET (AFTER EVERY USE)

1. While the skillet is still warm, wipe its inside surface with paper towels to remove excess food and oil.

2. Rinse the skillet under hot running water, scrubbing with a nonmetal brush or nonabrasive scrub pad to remove stubborn food.

3. Dry the skillet thoroughly by hand. Do not air-dry.

4. Heat the skillet over medium-low heat until all the moisture has evaporated.

5. Add ½ teaspoon of oil to the pan, using a paper towel to lightly coat its interior with oil.

6. Continue wiping until the skillet looks dark and smooth and no oil residue remains. Let the pan cool completely.

COOKING METHODS

There are so many delicious ways to prepare and serve meat. Let's look closer at the most common cooking methods, as well as best practices, to ensure stellar results and get the most out of your meats.

Braising

Braising is a cooking method that uses both wet and dry heat. Usually, food is first sautéed or seared at a high temperature. Then, a liquid—often wine, broth, or tomato sauce—is added. The dish is finished in a covered pot over low heat. This technique is most commonly used for tougher cuts of meat, such as chuck roast and shanks, as they rely on extra time and moisture to break down the tough connective tissue (collagen) that binds together the muscle fibers (aka "meat").

Frying

Cooking food in hot fat or oil—frying—is usually done with a shallow oil bath in a pan over a fire. Meanwhile, deep frying occurs when food is completely immersed in a deeper pot or vessel containing hot oil.

Grilling

Grilling is a style of cooking in which direct, radiant, dry heat is applied to the surface of food, either from above, from the side, or from below.

Marinating

Marinating is the process of soaking foods in a flavored liquid before cooking them. In addition to infusing the meat with flavor, marinating helps make your food more moist and tenderizes tougher cuts, a benefit that carries through the cooking process.

Pan-Roasting

Pan-roasting refers to a dual technique of cooking. First, the dish is partly cooked in a pan over direct heat, usually to get the outside crispy. Then, the pan is transferred to the oven to finish cooking.

Pan-Searing

Pan-searing (or searing) is a technique in which the surface of food is cooked at a high temperature until a brown crust forms.

Roasting

Roasting is a dry-heat cooking technique that relies on hot air to conduct heat and evenly brown the exterior of food on all sides. This hot air surrounds food at a temperature of at least 300°F, whether by oven, open flame, or another heat source.

Sautéing

Sautéing refers to the process of cooking food quickly in a small amount of fat over high heat.

FOOD SAFETY

Handling, preparing, and storing of food to prevent food poisoning and foodborne illness is an integral part of cooking, especially with meat and poultry. Here's what you need to know to keep you and your loved ones safe.

Cleaning the Refrigerator

Once per week, clear your refrigerator of food that should no longer be eaten. Cooked leftovers should be tossed after 4 days, while raw poultry and ground meat should be discarded after 2 days at most.

Cross Contamination

Separate foods when shopping and when chopping. Meat should be bagged separately from everything else, and it should be stored that way, too. If there are plastic bags available in the meat department, it's a good idea to use them for added protection. Be sure to always use a clean cutting board for fresh produce and a different one for raw seafood, meat, and poultry. Once food is cooked, never place it on the same plate or cutting board that previously held raw food. Likewise, always use clean utensils that have not previously touched raw meat.

Internal Cooking Temperatures

Use a food thermometer when cooking meat to ensure it has reached and maintains a safe temperature until eaten.

Beef: 115° to 120°F for rare; 120° to 125°F for medium-rare; 130° to 135°F for medium; 140° to 145°F for medium-well; and 150° to 155°F for well-done

Ground meat and meat mixtures: Beef, lamb, pork, and veal to 160°F and chicken or turkey to 165°F

Lamb: 145°F for medium-well

Pork: 145°F for medium-rare and 160°F for medium

Poultry: 165°F

Veal: 145°F for medium rare; 160°F for medium; and 170°F for well-done

Allow all meat to rest for at least 5 minutes before carving or eating (see "The Fundamentals of Cooking Meat," page 1).

Safe Storage Practices

It's important to heed expiration dates and watch for signs of spoilage. This includes slime, discoloration, and a bad smell for meat, seafood, and poultry. In the case of canned goods like chicken, tuna, corned beef, or anchovies, always throw out a can if it has a bulge or a dent, a strong smell upon opening, gas or spurting liquids, or a cloudy or mushy appearance.

Important as being diligent with food safety is, one question remains: What do the expiration labels *really* mean?

Best If Used By/Before: With the exception of infant formula, this is not an indicator of food safety. The date, which may appear on meat, poultry, or egg product labels, guarantees the food to be at the peak of its quality or flavor.

Sell By: This date is set by manufacturers to tell retailers when to remove the item from shelves. As such, it isn't a safety date. However, it is something to take seriously, since quality declines from there on out. After this date, you have several days to several weeks to use the product, though this depends entirely on the item itself. For instance, properly refrigerated milk should last 5 to 7 days beyond its sell-by date before it turns sour.

Freeze By: While not an indicator of food safety, this date tells you when a product should be frozen to maintain peak quality. Freezing does not destroy harmful germs, but it does keep food safe until it's thawed and cooked.

Perishable food should be refrigerated within 2 hours of purchase. The U.S. Food and Drug Administration's guidelines say that refrigerators should be set to 40°F or below and freezers to 0°F. Don't leave perishable foods out of the refrigerator for more than 2 hours. If food is exposed to temperatures above 90°F—such as in a hot car or at a summer picnic—refrigerate it within 1 hour.

Have leftovers? Place them in shallow containers, promptly refrigerating them for quick cooling. Never thaw or marinate foods on the counter; instead, thaw or marinate meat, poultry, and seafood in the refrigerator.

Finally, don't wash raw meat or poultry. Bacteria in the meat and poultry juices can be spread to other foods, surfaces, and utensils through cross-contamination.

Washing Hands, Utensils, Plates, and Surfaces

Before cooking, always wash your hands with soap and water, lathering up for at least 20 seconds. If possible, use a paper towel to turn off the faucet once you rinse. Hands should be rewashed each time you touch raw meat, poultry, and seafood. Additionally, surfaces should be washed with hot, soapy water.

By mixing ½ cup of unscented, liquid chlorine bleach with a gallon of water, you have a reliable, inexpensive disinfectant for nonporous countertops, sinks, floors, stainless steel appliances, refrigerators, and other hard surfaces. Do be aware that a bleach solution loses its potency over time, so discard after 24 hours.

Beyond regularly cleaning the inside and outside of your appliances, pay close attention to buttons and handles. It's important to clean them well to avoid cross-contamination.

2

BEEF

From burgers to braises, steaks to stir-fries, satisfying beef dishes abound. Whether it's a quick weeknight meal or a slow-simmered Sunday supper, this chapter showcases the wide array of ways to enjoy the meaty mainstay. Are you the type who wants Thai basil beef one night and *svíčková* the next? These recipes will whisk you to faraway places sans plane ticket.

⟵≪ GRILLED CHIMICHURRI FLANK STEAK, PAGE 34

COMMON CUTS

When selecting beef, chilled meat should be dry and firm to the touch. It should never be wet or wobbly. Avoid meat that is grayish in color or brown around the edges. In the case of high-quality steaks and roasts, look for meat that is deep red with good, even marbling. These qualities result in juicier, richer meat.

Brisket

Among the tougher, leaner cuts of beef, brisket hails from the breast area, behind the front leg. Ideal for slow-and-low cooking, it comes in two cuts: flat cut (also called first cut) or point cut. Thicker and more flavorful, the point cut features a layer of fat. It's best suited for smoking or braising, as well as stewing on the stovetop or in the oven. Purchase point cut brisket if you can, though it's not always available at a standard supermarket.

Chuck Roast

Commonly referred to as pot roast, the coarse-grained chuck roast comes from the large, square shoulder portion of the steer. The chuck roast is relatively inexpensive and definitely flavorful, with a lot of connective tissue running through it. As such, it calls for braising and stewing. Stew meat is cut from the chuck.

Filet Mignon

Also known as tenderloin steak, this luxe, lean cut comes from the long, supple loin. Weighing between 7 and 15 pounds when whole, it's a prized cut from a 1,000-plus-pound steer and should be deep red in color and carefully, evenly cut. Best when simply seasoned with salt and pepper or a rub, it should be cooked 3 to 4 minutes per side on the grill or seared 4 to 5 minutes per side in a pan for medium-rare.

Flank Steak

This long, flat cut hails from the belly muscle. Featuring a vertical grain, it's chewy unless properly prepared. Do not overcook it. Slice it thin against the grain when serving. It's best when marinated for a least an hour (or overnight), simply seasoned with salt and pepper, or slathered with a rub. For medium-rare flank steak, grill it for 4 to 5 minutes per side, sear it for 5 to 6 minutes per side, or broil it for 6 to 7 minutes per side.

Ground Beef

A mixture of ground meat and fat, ground beef is labeled by its lean-to-fat ratio. For example, 80 / 20 means it consists of 80 percent lean beef to 20 percent fat.

- **Ground chuck:** 80 percent lean / 20 percent fat
- **Ground round:** 85 percent lean / 15 percent fat
- **Ground sirloin:** 90 percent lean / 10 percent fat

Ground beef is best panfried, grilled, roasted, and broiled. Be sure to purchase bright red meat. A higher fat content yields juicier results.

New York Strip, Porterhouse, Rib Eye, Prime Rib, and Sirloin

Also called shell steak, top loin steak, and Kansas City strip, **New York strip** is cut from the top of the short loin. This cut is best seasoned with salt and pepper or rubbed with a seasoning mixture. For medium-rare, grill it for 3 to 4 minutes per side or sear it for 4 to 5 minutes per side. When the cut includes both strip steak and filet mignon, it's called a **porterhouse**. Sometimes called Delmonico steak or (when bone-in) rib steak, the marbled, full-bodied **rib eye** comes from the top of the steer's rib section, its most tender. Season with salt and pepper or use a rub. Then, for a medium-rare steak, grill for 2 to 3 minutes per side or sear it 3 to 4 minutes per side. **Prime rib** ("standing rib roast") is also cut from the rib section of the steer and often contains large sections of the rib bone. Standing rib roasts, as the name suggests, are ideal for roasting. **Sirloin,** also called top sirloin steak and sirloin butt steak, is cut from the area between the short loin and round. Look for steaks labeled "top sirloin" over "bottom sirloin." To prepare the meat, season with salt and pepper, use a rub, or marinate. Then, for a medium-rare sirloin, grill it for 3 to 4 minutes per side or sear it 4 to 5 minutes per side.

Short Ribs

Blocky and rectangular, short ribs are 2 to 3 inches long and hail from the chuck, loin, or mid-rib area. Ribbons of meat and fat lend deep, rich flavor to this tough cut, which benefits from long, slow, covered braising.

Skirt Steak

Skirt steak comes from the steer's plate section and is also referred to as Romanian steak and Philadelphia steak. The long, thin, narrow cut averages 12 to 15 inches and is sometimes sold in pieces. Season with salt and pepper, use a rub, or marinate the meat. For medium-rare, grill it for 1 to 3 minutes per side or sear it 2 to 4 minutes per side.

Top Round

The lean, boneless, juicy top round or London broil comes from the rear of the steer. Marinate it to tenderize the meat before grilling 4 to 5 minutes per side, searing 5 to 6 minutes per side, or broiling 6 to 7 minutes per side for medium-rare. Then, slice it thin.

Tri-Tip

Also called Newport steak, triangle steak, or bottom sirloin steak, this triangular cut comes from the bottom sirloin section of the steer. Given that it's extra-thick, it needs to be covered when grilled. Simply season with salt and pepper, use a rub, or marinate the meat. Then, three good options are to grill it for 8 to 10 minutes per side over medium heat; sear it in a pan for 4 to 5 minutes per side, then roast at 450°F for an additional 8 to 10 minutes to get the right internal temperature; or broil it for 10 to 12 minutes per side.

WHAT COULD GO WRONG?

Q: Why should I salt and season beef generously?
You can't season a steak's interior, so it's important to season meat well on both sides 30 minutes prior to cooking. This will bring out its rich flavor and help build a crust.

Q: Can I cook steak when it's cold?
Giving meat time to reach room temperature helps prevent it from cooking unevenly. Take it out of the refrigerator at least 30 minutes before cooking. But don't worry—it won't kill you! Taking the chill off your roasts, pork chops, and even fish prior to cooking produces juicier, more evenly cooked meat.

Q: Why is my meat so chewy?
Treating cuts of beef as if they're the same can deprive you of flavor and land you with a tough or dried-out meal. Make sure you understand the cuts, as well as their ideal cooking techniques.

Q: When cooking a steak, do I only turn it once?
Contrary to conventional wisdom, turning a steak just once has the potential to dry it out. Instead, it's best to flip a steak using tongs once every minute or two throughout cooking, especially when it's cooked over high heat. Doing so results in a juicier steak with less curling at the edges.

Q: Can I slice meat right after it comes off the heat?
Never cut into meat too soon, as it needs time to rest. When cooked, the meat fibers shrink. Letting meat rest gives the fibers time to expand and reabsorb the juices (see "The Fundamentals of Cooking Meat," page 1).

Q: What's the difference between tender cuts and tougher cuts?
Tender cuts like filet mignon and strip steak have little connective tissue and can take high, dry heat. They're best-suited to quick cooking styles, such as pan-searing, grilling, and frying. Larger tender cuts like prime rib are ideal for roasting. In contrast, tougher cuts have a lot of connective tissue and therefore require moist, slow, and low cooking to break down the connective tissue and transform it into a juicy, succulent meal.

Pan-Seared Steak with Red-Eye Gravy

ONE POT

A Southern favorite that typically features ham slices, this beefy interpretation gains smokiness from rendered bacon fat, depth from unsweetened cocoa powder, and a silky texture courtesy of a pat of butter.

Serves 4

PREP TIME:
15 minutes

COOK TIME:
20 minutes

4 (4-ounce) rib eye steaks
1 teaspoon kosher salt
½ teaspoon freshly ground black pepper
2 hardwood-smoked bacon slices

½ cup brewed coffee
¼ cup beef broth
½ teaspoon unsweetened cocoa powder
½ teaspoon all-purpose flour
2 tablespoons unsalted butter

1. Place the steaks between 2 sheets of heavy-duty plastic wrap and flatten to ¼-inch thickness using a rolling pin or the flat side of a meat mallet. Season the steaks with salt and pepper.

2. In a large skillet over medium-high heat, cook the bacon until crispy. Remove and discard (or save) the bacon, leaving the fat. Add the steaks to the hot pan and fry until nicely browned, about 2 minutes per side.

3. Transfer the steaks to a platter and tent with aluminum foil to keep warm. Add the coffee and beef broth to the pan and simmer, scraping up browned bits as you stir. Reduce the heat to medium-low. Whisk in the cocoa powder and flour and add the butter. Simmer until the sauce is reduced by half and slightly thickened, about 5 minutes.

4. Drizzle the sauce over the reserved steaks and serve.

> **PREP TIP**: The steaks can be pounded, seasoned, and individually sealed in plastic wrap to store in the refrigerator for up to 4 hours in advance.

Spicy Thai-Inspired Basil Beef

A stir-fry with basil is a staple of Thai cuisine, and it's among my weeknight go-tos. Preparing it with ground beef makes it an effortless one-pot meal the whole family can enjoy. Another plus? It's riff-able and made largely from pantry items you might have on hand.

 Serves 4

PREP TIME:
15 minutes

COOK TIME:
15 minutes

1 pound ground beef

1 red, orange, or yellow bell pepper, thinly sliced

2 bird's-eye chiles or jalapeños, finely sliced (optional)

1 small onion, thinly sliced

5 garlic cloves, minced

1 tablespoon soy sauce

1 teaspoon oyster sauce

1 tablespoon fish sauce

½ teaspoon palm sugar or light brown sugar, packed

¾ cup fresh basil or Thai basil leaves, packed

1 cup cooked white rice, for serving

½ lime, cut into wedges

1. In a large skillet or wok over medium-high heat, brown the ground beef, breaking it into small bits until cooked through. Push the beef to the side of the skillet.

2. Add the bell pepper, chiles, and onion, and cook for 2 minutes. Add the garlic and cook for 1 minute more before adding the soy, oyster, and fish sauces, as well as the palm sugar. Stir-fry for 30 seconds. Fold in the basil, cooking just until it wilts.

3. Remove from the heat and serve on rice with the lime wedges.

> **INGREDIENT TIP:** If you use sweet basil instead of the Thai variety, be prepared to tear the larger leaves into manageable, bite-size pieces.

All-In-One Grilled or Baked Burger Packets

MAKE AHEAD · ONE POT

I was a Brownie and, for a brief while, a Girl Scout. My favorite part? Going on campouts so I could cook over an open fire. Try this on your next camping excursion, at a backyard barbecue, or on a cold winter night when you're hankering for warm weather.

Serves 4

PREP TIME:
15 minutes

COOK TIME:
30 minutes,
plus 5 minutes
to rest

1 pound ground sirloin, at least 90 percent lean

1 packet onion soup mix, such as Lipton

¼ cup finely chopped onion

1 large egg, whisked

2 tablespoons bread crumbs

1½ teaspoons Worcestershire sauce

½ teaspoon kosher salt

½ teaspoon freshly ground black pepper

8 ounces baby portabella or white button mushrooms, quartered

¼ cup ketchup

2 teaspoons yellow mustard

2 ounces processed cheese, such as Velveeta, cubed

½ teaspoon seasoned salt, such as Lawry's

1. Light a charcoal grill or heat a gas grill to medium-high (375°F). If you don't have a grill, adjust the oven rack to a lower-middle position and preheat the oven to 375°F.

2. On a large work surface, lay two long, intersecting pieces of foil to form a large "plus" sign. In a large bowl, combine the beef, soup mix, onion, egg, bread crumbs, Worcestershire sauce, salt, and pepper. Mix gently with your hands until combined. Don't over-mix. Form into four even patties and place the meat on top of the foil.

3. Top the patties with mushrooms, ketchup, mustard, cheese, and seasoned salt. Seal packet completely so no liquid can escape.

4. Put on the grill or, if using the oven, in an 18-by-13-inch baking sheet. Cook for about 30 minutes, flipping halfway through, until the meat reaches an internal temperature of 130°F for medium-rare or 140°F for medium. Remove from the heat and allow the meat to rest for 5 minutes. Serve right from the foil.

> **PREP TIP:** The burger packets can be prepared and stored in the refrigerator up to 1 day in advance.

Classic Sloppy Joes

Classic sloppy joes are easy to make from scratch, and the meat mixture stores well in the refrigerator. I like my joes topped with a slice of American cheese, pickle "coins," and a handful of potato chips.

Serves 4

PREP TIME:
5 minutes

COOK TIME:
25 minutes

1 pound lean ground beef

1 medium onion, finely chopped

⅔ cup ketchup

1½ tablespoons yellow mustard

1 tablespoon light brown sugar, packed

2 teaspoons distilled white vinegar

½ teaspoon Worcestershire sauce

½ teaspoon garlic powder

¼ cup water

4 store-bought hamburger buns

1. In a large skillet over medium-high heat, brown the ground beef, breaking it into small, even chunks until cooked through and lightly caramelized. Nudge the beef off to one side, reduce the heat to medium, and add the onion. Cook, stirring often, until the onion is soft and translucent, about 7 minutes.

2. Add the ketchup, mustard, brown sugar, vinegar, Worcestershire sauce, garlic powder, and water, and stir to combine. Continue cooking for 5 minutes.

3. Serve on hamburger buns.

SUBSTITUTION TIP: Don't have ketchup? Try barbecue sauce instead. Like heat? Add a few dashes of hot sauce or ¼ teaspoon of red pepper flakes.

Panfried Wisconsin Butter Burgers

Family owned and operated since 1936, Milwaukee's iconic Solly's Grille serves a storied version of this proverbial heart-attack-on-a-plate, topped with stewed onions and cheese. In your own home and at Solly's, know that this will be a "many napkins" affair.

Serves 4

PREP TIME:
10 minutes

COOK TIME:
45 minutes

1 pound ground sirloin
¾ teaspoon kosher salt, plus more to season
½ teaspoon freshly ground black pepper, plus more to season
5 tablespoons unsalted butter, room temperature, divided

1 tablespoon extra-virgin olive oil
2 medium onions, diced
½ cup dry white wine, such as pinot grigio
1 cup beef broth
4 hamburger buns
4 slices American cheese

1. In a medium bowl, combine the ground sirloin, salt, and pepper, taking care not to over-mix. Form the mixture into four patties and transfer to the refrigerator until ready to use.

2. In a medium skillet over low heat, add 2 tablespoons of the butter and the olive oil. When the butter is melted and the oil hot, add the onions and wine and cook for 10 minutes, or until the onions are translucent, stirring occasionally so they don't caramelize. Add the beef broth. Season with salt and pepper and cover, cooking for 20 minutes and stirring occasionally. Remove the lid, raise the heat to medium-high, and continue cooking until the liquid evaporates. Remove the skillet from the heat and allow the mixture to cool to room temperature.

3. Use 1 tablespoon of butter to slather the insides of the hamburger buns. In a large skillet over medium-high heat, quickly toast the buttered buns. Remove and reserve.

Continued ☞

4. In the same large skillet, melt the remaining 2 tablespoons of butter. When the butter is sizzling, add the reserved patties. Season lightly with salt. Flip when the juices start bubbling up through the top of the meat, about 4 minutes. Spread the onion mixture evenly over the top of the patties. Top each with a slice of cheese. Cover and cook until the cheese melts, about 1 minute.

5. Transfer the patties to the waiting buns and serve with your condiments of choice.

PREP TIP: The onions can be prepared up to 3 days in advance. Store them in an airtight container in the refrigerator until you're ready to use them.

Bacon-Wrapped, Cheese-Stuffed Meat Loaf

MAKE AHEAD

Meat loaf is an all-American dish that can be enjoyed "hot off the presses" or sliced, rewarmed, and turned into a sandwich the next day. Or prepare it in advance: Stop just short of cooking it and refrigerate for up to a day.

 Serves 4

PREP TIME:
15 minutes

COOK TIME:
30 minutes,
plus 5 minutes
to rest

Nonstick cooking spray
1 pound ground beef
½ pound ground pork
1 egg, lightly beaten
¾ cup quick-cooking oats, dry
2 large garlic cloves, minced
1 packet onion soup mix, such as Lipton
1½ tablespoons tomato paste

1 teaspoon kosher salt
½ teaspoon freshly ground black pepper
½ cup ketchup
2 tablespoons homemade or store-bought barbecue sauce
¾ cup shredded sharp cheddar cheese
4 bacon slices, halved

1. Preheat the oven to 350°F. Line an 18-by-13-inch baking sheet with foil and spray with nonstick cooking spray.

2. In a large bowl, add the beef, pork, egg, oats, garlic, soup mix, tomato paste, salt, and pepper and mix with hands until combined. Do not over-mix.

3. In a small bowl, combine the ketchup and barbecue sauce and set aside. Divide the cheese into four equal portions.

4. Form four individual, oblong meat loaves, putting the portioned-out cheese in the middle of each loaf and enclosing the meat around the cheese. Top each meat loaf with an "X" using the bacon halves. Slather generously with the ketchup-barbecue glaze.

5. Place the meat loaves on the prepared baking sheet and transfer to the oven to bake until the bacon is browned and crispy and the meat registers 155°F on an instant-read thermometer when inserted into the middle of the meat loaf, about 25 to 30 minutes. Let rest for 5 minutes before serving.

SUBSTITUTION TIP: Don't have barbecue sauce? Replace it with sriracha for a spicy twist. Want a crusty glaze? Try zigzagging some honey on top.

Umami-Packed Cottage Pie

FREEZER-FRIENDLY · MAKE AHEAD

Few things are more comforting than a serving of shepherd's pie. This version, called "cottage pie" because it's made with beef instead of lamb, gets its umami from the addition of tomato paste, mustard, and Parmesan. And, if you happen to have any in your pantry, try adding 2 teaspoons of fish sauce to the mix.

Serves 6

PREP TIME:
30 minutes

COOK TIME:
1 hour
50 minutes,
plus
15 minutes
to rest

FOR THE POTATOES

5 medium Yukon Gold potatoes, peeled and cut into chunks
3 tablespoons unsalted butter
⅓ cup grated Parmesan cheese

¼ cup milk
½ teaspoon kosher salt
½ teaspoon freshly ground black pepper

FOR THE FILLING

½ tablespoon extra-virgin olive oil
1½ pounds ground beef
1 medium onion, minced
1 celery stalk, finely chopped
2 medium garlic cloves, minced
2 large eggs
1 tablespoon Worcestershire sauce
1 tablespoon Dijon mustard
1½ tablespoons tomato paste
½ teaspoon smoked paprika

¾ teaspoon dried thyme
⅓ cup finely crushed saltine crackers
⅓ cup finely grated Parmesan cheese
¾ cup frozen peas and carrots mixture, thawed
¾ teaspoon kosher salt
½ teaspoon freshly ground black pepper
Nonstick cooking spray
2 tablespoons unsalted butter

TO MAKE THE POTATOES

1. In a large saucepan over medium-high heat, cover the potatoes with water and bring to a boil. Reduce the heat to medium-low and simmer until tender, about 20 minutes.

2. Drain the potatoes and return them to the pan, adding the butter, Parmesan, milk, salt, and pepper. Using a handheld mixer or fork, whip the potatoes, being careful not to over-mix.

TO MAKE THE FILLING

3. Adjust the oven rack to the lower-middle position and preheat the oven to 375°F.

4. In a large skillet over medium heat, heat the oil until it shimmers. Brown the ground beef, breaking it into small bits, until cooked through. Push the beef to the side of the pan. Add the onion, celery, and garlic and cook, stirring often, until tender and translucent, about 7 minutes. Combine the beef with the onion mixture and allow it to cool.

5. In a large bowl, whisk the eggs. Add the meat mixture, Worcestershire sauce, mustard, tomato paste, paprika, thyme, crackers, Parmesan, peas and carrots mixture, salt, and pepper. Gently combine.

6. Spray an 8-by-8-inch baking dish with nonstick cooking spray. Pack the meat mixture lightly into the pan. Evenly spread the potato mixture on top and make a crosshatch pattern in it using the tines of a fork. Cut the butter into small pieces and dot them across the top of the potatoes. Transfer to the oven to bake until the internal temperature on a meat thermometer inserted into the center of the beef reaches 135° to 140°F, about 55 minutes to 1 hour and 5 minutes.

7. Remove from the oven and allow the meat to rest for 15 minutes before serving.

> **STORAGE TIP**: If you plan to freeze the cottage pie, replace the milk in the potatoes with heavy cream. After baking, let the baking dish cool to room temperature. Cover tightly with foil and place in the freezer for up to 2 months. When ready to eat, preheat the oven to 350°F. Transfer the cottage pie to the oven and bake for 1 hour, still covered with foil. If you thaw the pie in the refrigerator the night before, reduce the cooking time to about 30 to 35 minutes, or until the internal temperature on a meat thermometer reaches 135° to 140°F.

Beefy, Cheesy Stuffed Peppers

FREEZER-FRIENDLY · MAKE AHEAD

This childhood favorite gets a reboot with a cheesy filling and punchy tomato sauce. Serve it with a crisp, lightly dressed salad. And don't forget to save leftovers, because this dish reheats—and freezes—well.

Serves 4

PREP TIME:
20 minutes

COOK TIME:
1 hour
30 minutes,
plus
10 minutes
to rest

FOR THE SAUCE

2 (15-ounce) cans tomato sauce
½ teaspoon garlic powder
½ teaspoon onion powder
½ teaspoon kosher salt
½ teaspoon balsamic vinegar
½ teaspoon freshly
  ground black pepper

FOR THE PEPPERS

1 tablespoon extra-virgin
  olive oil
1 pound ground beef
1 medium onion, finely chopped
2 medium garlic cloves, minced
½ teaspoon seasoned salt
2 cups cooked white rice
1 cup canned crushed tomatoes
1½ teaspoons
  Worcestershire sauce
½ cup shredded sharp
  cheddar cheese
2 slices American cheese, cubed
¾ teaspoon kosher salt
½ teaspoon freshly
  ground black pepper
4 large red, yellow, or
  orange bell peppers

TO MAKE THE SAUCE

1. In a small saucepan over medium heat, stir to combine the tomato sauce, garlic powder, onion powder, salt, balsamic vinegar, and pepper. Bring to a low boil and allow to simmer for 10 minutes, stirring occasionally. Remove from the heat and set aside.

TO MAKE THE PEPPERS

2. Adjust the oven rack to the lower-middle position and preheat the oven to 350°F.

3. In a large skillet, heat the oil over medium-high heat until shimmering. Add the beef and brown, breaking into small bits, until cooked through. Add the onion and continue cooking for 4 minutes until it

is just beginning to soften. Stir in the garlic and cook for 1 minute. Add the seasoned salt, rice, tomatoes, Worcestershire sauce, sharp cheddar cheese, American cheese, salt, and pepper, and bring to a simmer. Taste and adjust the seasoning, if needed. Continue cooking until the cheese is melted and the filling is creamy, about 5 minutes longer. Remove from the heat.

4. Slice off the tops of the peppers, remove the seeds and membranes, and trim the bottoms so the peppers can stand upright.

5. Arrange the peppers cut-side up in an 8-by-8-inch baking dish. Generously stuff the peppers with the filling and ladle the sauce on top. Cover the pan with foil and bake, basting with sauce every 15 minutes, until the peppers are tender, about 1 hour. Remove the foil during the last 15 minutes of cooking.

6. Remove from oven and let peppers rest for 10 minutes before serving.

Grilled Chimichurri Flank Steak

FREEZER-FRIENDLY · MAKE AHEAD

When my family fired up the grill when I was young, it always felt like a celebration. In my household, flank steak was a real crowd-pleaser. It's no wonder, since it picks up the flavor of a marinade—in this case, fresh, herby chimichurri, a staple in Argentina and Uruguay—in no time.

Serves 6

PREP TIME:
20 minutes, plus 4 hours to marinate

COOK TIME:
15 minutes, plus 5 minutes to rest

½ cup finely chopped fresh flat-leaf parsley

4 tablespoons fresh, finely chopped oregano

4½ tablespoons capers, drained and roughly chopped

2 tablespoons finely chopped red onion

4 garlic cloves, peeled and minced

4 tablespoons extra-virgin olive oil, divided

4 tablespoons red wine vinegar

½ teaspoon red pepper flakes

½ teaspoon kosher salt

1 whole flank steak (about 2½ pounds)

1. In a medium bowl, combine the parsley, oregano, capers, onion, garlic, 3 tablespoons of the olive oil, red wine vinegar, red pepper flakes, and salt. Taste and adjust the seasoning, if needed.

2. Place the flank steak in a large, resealable bag. Add half the chimichurri, seal the bag tightly, and squish the contents around to distribute the marinade. Transfer the meat to the refrigerator and marinate for 4 hours or overnight. Refrigerate the remaining chimichurri until ready to use.

3. Light a charcoal grill, heat a gas grill to medium-high (375°F), or heat a grill pan over medium-high heat on the stovetop. Remove the steak from the marinade and pat dry with paper towels. Cook the steak until well charred, about 5 minutes. Flip the steak and continue cooking until the second side has a nice crust as well, another 5 minutes.

4. Reduce the heat if cooking on the stovetop or transfer the steak to a cooler area of the grill. Cook until the center of the steak registers 130°F on an instant-read thermometer for medium-rare or 135°F for medium, about 5 minutes longer. Transfer to a cutting board, tent the steak with foil, and allow it to rest for at least 5 minutes.

5. Slice the steak thinly across the grain. Serve with reserved chimichurri.

PREP TIP: The steak can be marinated and frozen in an airtight bag for up to 3 months. Thaw before cooking. The chimichurri can also be made ahead of time and kept in the refrigerator for a week.

Tangy, Braised Beef Brisket

FREEZER-FRIENDLY · MAKE AHEAD · ONE POT

Cooked with an obscene amount of sliced onions, this flavorful brisket can be made ahead. Make the dish and transfer it to the refrigerator overnight to deepen its flavor. It's well worth the added time, if you don't need to eat the brisket the same day.

PREP TIME:
20 minutes

COOK TIME:
4 hours
30 minutes

1 (5- to 6-pound) beef brisket, point cut or flat cut, trimmed of fat
Kosher salt, divided
Freshly ground black pepper, divided
1½ tablespoons extra-virgin olive oil
8 medium yellow onions, sliced ½-inch thick
2 garlic cloves, minced

¼ cup dry red wine
2 (14.5-ounce) cans fire-roasted diced tomatoes with their juices
1 tablespoon light brown sugar, packed
1½ tablespoons balsamic vinegar
1 tablespoon Worcestershire sauce
6 carrots, halved lengthwise

1. Preheat the oven to 350°F. Season the brisket with salt and pepper.

2. In a large Dutch oven over medium-high heat on the stovetop, heat the oil until shimmering. Add the brisket and brown on both sides, 8 to 10 minutes total. Remove from the Dutch oven and reserve.

3. Reduce the heat to medium. Add the onions and sauté, scraping up browned bits from the bottom of the pan and stirring occasionally, until the onions are translucent and tender, about 7 minutes. Add the garlic and continue cooking for 30 seconds, then add the red wine. After 2 minutes, add the tomatoes, brown sugar, balsamic vinegar, and Worcestershire sauce. Season with salt and pepper, return the meat to the Dutch oven, and spoon the sauce on top of the meat. Scatter the carrots throughout. Bring to a low boil.

4. Cover and transfer to the oven to cook for 1½ hours. Remove the meat and transfer to a cutting board. Cut across the grain into ⅛-inch-thick slices. Nestle the meat back into the Dutch oven, spooning the sauce on top.

5. Reduce the oven to 325°F and continue cooking for 1½ to 2½ hours, or until the meat is fork-tender. Baste the meat every 30 minutes, adding a few tablespoons of water if the sauce begins to look dry.

6. Remove from the oven, taste, and adjust seasoning, if needed. Serve or transfer to the refrigerator for a day so the flavors have a chance to meld.

PREP TIP: You can prepare the brisket through step 2 and transfer to the bowl of a slow cooker, cooking over low heat for 8 to 10 hours. Slice meat halfway through and continue cooking as directed.

Czech Svíčková

Growing up in Chicago's western suburbs, I was blessed with access to great, stick-to-your-ribs Czech/Bohemian–inspired fare. This indulgent, heart-warming dish tops my list. Serve it with bread dumplings.

Serves 6

PREP TIME:
30 minutes

COOK TIME:
3 hours
20 minutes

2-pound beef sirloin roast (or rump roast)

½ teaspoon kosher salt

½ teaspoon freshly ground black pepper

2 slices hardwood-smoked bacon

1 large carrot, sliced

1 medium celery root, peeled and diced

1 medium parsnip, peeled and diced

1 large onion, chopped

10 black peppercorns

4 allspice berries

2 dried bay leaves

1 cup low-sodium beef broth

2 tablespoons freshly squeezed lemon juice

1 teaspoon white vinegar

2 tablespoons butter, melted

1 cup heavy cream

2½ tablespoons all-purpose flour

1½ teaspoons sugar

1. Preheat the oven to 325°F. Season the roast with salt and pepper.

2. In a large Dutch oven over medium-high heat on the stovetop, cook the bacon until it is crispy, about 10 minutes. Remove and discard (or save) the bacon, leaving the fat. Brown the roast all over in hot bacon fat, about 3 minutes per side.

3. Add the carrot, celery root, parsnip, onion, peppercorns, allspice berries, bay leaves, broth, lemon juice, and white vinegar to the Dutch oven and stir to combine. Pour the melted butter on top. Cover and transfer to the oven to cook for 2 to 3 hours, basting occasionally, until the meat is fork-tender.

4. Remove from the oven, transfer the Dutch oven to the stovetop, and discard the bay leaves. Transfer the meat to a cutting board, tenting it with foil.

5. In a blender, puree the sauce and vegetables from the Dutch oven until smooth. Return the puree to the pot. Whisk the heavy cream with the flour, then add the sugar to the mixture. Add the cream mixture to the puree in the pot. Stir, taste, and adjust seasoning, if needed.

6. Slice the meat and serve atop sauce.

PREP TIP: You can prepare the recipe through the second step and transfer it to the bowl of a slow cooker, cooking over low heat for 8 to 10 hours. To finish the sauce, continue cooking for 30 minutes after adding the heavy cream.

Grilled Teriyaki Strip Steak

Sweet, salty, and caramelized, these marinated strip steaks are perfect for a backyard barbecue, served alongside rice and cold sake. Leftovers can be tucked into wraps with lettuce and matchstick-cut carrots, cucumbers, and pears.

Serves 4

PREP TIME:
10 minutes,
plus 4 hours to
marinate

COOK TIME:
35 minutes,
plus 5 minutes
to rest

2 cups soy sauce
1 tablespoon honey
¾ cup granulated sugar
1 tablespoon light brown
 sugar, packed
2 large garlic cloves, minced
¼ cup minced onion
1 tablespoon grated ginger

1 teaspoon garlic powder
¼ cup sesame seeds, toasted
1 tablespoon cornstarch
 dissolved in ¼ cup water
4 (1½-inch thick) strip steaks
Nonstick cooking
 spray (optional)

1. In a medium saucepan over low heat, combine the soy sauce, honey, granulated sugar, brown sugar, garlic, onion, ginger, garlic powder, and sesame seeds and simmer for 15 minutes. Whisk in the cornstarch and continue cooking, stirring constantly, until thickened, about 3 minutes. Let the sauce cool.

2. Place the strip steaks in a large, resealable bag. Add half of the teriyaki sauce. Seal the bag and squish the contents around to evenly distribute the marinade. Refrigerate the remaining sauce in an airtight container. Transfer the steaks to the refrigerator to marinate for at least 4 hours or overnight.

3. Light a charcoal grill or heat a gas grill to medium-high heat (375°F). Alternatively, spray a grill pan with nonstick cooking spray and heat it on medium-high heat on the stovetop. Remove the meat from the marinade and pat dry with paper towels. Place the steaks on a cooler area of the grill. Cook, flipping the meat and taking the temperature every few minutes to prevent burning, 10 to 15 minutes. When the steaks register 115°F for medium-rare or 125°F for medium on an instant-read thermometer, transfer to the hot area of the grill to lightly char for 1 minute on each side.

4. Remove steaks from the grill, tent with foil, and let rest for 5 minutes. Serve with reserved sauce.

Ropa Vieja

FREEZER-FRIENDLY · MAKE AHEAD · ONE POT

I was fortunate enough to travel to Cuba in 2012. While exploring the island's culinary traditions, I learned how to make this iconic dish in a local home. My advice: Make a big batch and freeze it in an airtight container for up to 3 months. I like serving mine with wedges of lime.

Serves 6

PREP TIME:
15 minutes

COOK TIME:
2 hours
15 minutes

2 pounds flank steak

¾ teaspoon kosher salt, plus extra for seasoning the steak

½ teaspoon freshly ground black pepper, plus extra for seasoning the steak

1 tablespoon extra-virgin olive oil

1 cup low-sodium beef broth

1 (14.5-ounce) can crushed tomatoes with their juices

1 (6-ounce) can tomato paste

1 medium onion, thinly sliced

1 large red pepper, thinly sliced

3 medium garlic cloves, minced

1 teaspoon ground cumin

½ cup sliced, pimento-stuffed Spanish (green) olives

1½ tablespoons olive brine

4 cups cooked white rice, for serving

1. Preheat the oven to 325°F. Season the meat generously with salt and pepper.

2. In a large Dutch oven on the stovetop, heat the oil over high heat, until shimmering. Add the flank steak and cook until well browned, about 3 minutes per side.

3. Add the broth, tomatoes, tomato paste, onion, red pepper, garlic, cumin, salt, and pepper and stir to combine. Bring to a boil. Cover and transfer to the oven to cook for 2 hours or until the meat is fork-tender.

4. Remove from the oven. Transfer the meat from the Dutch oven to a cutting board. Shred the meat using two forks.

5. Add the olives and olive brine to the sauce and stir to combine. Taste and adjust the seasoning, if needed. Return the meat to the Dutch oven and simmer over medium heat for 10 minutes to allow the flavors to combin. Serve with the rice.

PREP TIP: This recipe can be adapted for a slow cooker. Set it on low and cook until tender, about 8 hours. Shred the meat and proceed as directed.

Roasted Herb and Pepper-Crusted Eye of Round Roast

ONE POT

As simple as this roast is, it feels like a meal for a special occasion. Plus, leftover ribbons of thinly sliced beef are perfect for tucking into sandwiches, slathered with a dollop of horseradish sauce. You can also chop leftover meat and panfry it for tacos or a hash.

Serves 8

PREP TIME:
10 minutes

COOK TIME:
1 hour
10 minutes,
plus
10 minutes to
rest

1 (3½-pound) beef eye of round roast, trimmed of fat
1 teaspoon kosher salt
½ teaspoon freshly ground black pepper
2½ tablespoons extra-virgin olive oil, divided
½ teaspoon dried thyme
1 tablespoon dried marjoram
½ teaspoon dried oregano
½ teaspoon garlic powder
1 tablespoon grainy mustard, such as Maille Old Style Mustard

1. Preheat the oven to 375°F. Season the roast with salt and pepper.

2. In a small bowl, combine 1 tablespoon of olive oil with the thyme, marjoram, oregano, garlic powder, and mustard, mixing to form a paste. Rub the paste over the meat.

3. In a Dutch oven over medium-high heat on the stovetop, heat the remaining 1½ tablespoons of oil until shimmering. Add the roast and sear until well browned on all sides, about 8 minutes total.

4. Transfer the roast to the oven and bake until an instant-read thermometer inserted in the center reads 125°F for medium-rare or 135°F for medium, about 1 hour. Remove, transfer to a cutting board, and let rest for 10 minutes.

5. Slice and serve drizzled with pan juices.

> **SUBSTITUTION TIP:** Feel free to substitute an herb mixture of your choice, such as herbes de Provence or Italian seasoning.

Carne Asada

FREEZER-FRIENDLY · MAKE AHEAD

Carne asada is a wonderful dish to share at a backyard gathering. Serve a platter of the smoky, citrusy beef alongside warm tortillas, lime wedges, salsas, beans, and rice for a customizable, family-style meal.

PREP TIME:
15 minutes, plus 4 hours to marinate

COOK TIME:
20 minutes, plus 10 minutes to rest

2½ pounds flank steak
Juice of 1 orange
Juice of 2 limes
3 garlic cloves, smashed
½ teaspoon kosher salt, plus more to season
½ teaspoon freshly ground black pepper, plus more to season

1 medium onion, sliced
1 teaspoon ground cumin
¼ cup light Mexican lager, such as Corona or Modelo
2 tablespoons Worcestershire sauce
2 tablespoons vegetable oil
Nonstick cooking spray (optional)

1. Add the steak, orange juice, lime juice, garlic, salt, pepper, onion, cumin, lager, Worcestershire sauce, and oil to a large, resealable bag. Seal the bag and squish the contents around to combine the ingredients and distribute the liquid. Place on a plate and transfer to the refrigerator to marinate for 4 hours or overnight.

2. Light a charcoal grill or heat a gas grill to medium-high heat (375°F). Alternatively, spray a grill pan with nonstick cooking spray and heat it on medium-high heat on the stovetop. When sizzling hot, sear the steak on the hottest part of the grill, 3 minutes per side.

3. When the meat is nicely browned with a good crust, place it over indirect heat if grilling or reduce the heat to medium if using a gas grill or grill pan. Continue cooking until the center of the steak registers 125°F on an instant-read thermometer for medium-rare or 135°F for medium, 5 to 7 minutes more.

4. Transfer the meat to a cutting board, tenting it with foil and allowing it to rest for 10 minutes.

5. Thinly slice against the grain and serve.

Grilled Beef Shish Kebab

Variations of "meat and vegetables on a skewer" appear worldwide because, let's face it, meat on a skewer is fun and delicious. Feel free to customize your own shish kebab with whatever vegetables you think would work.

Serves 4

PREP TIME:
15 minutes, plus 4 hours to marinate

COOK TIME:
10 minutes, plus 5 minutes to rest

FOR THE MARINADE

⅓ cup vegetable oil

2 tablespoons soy sauce

1 tablespoon red wine vinegar

¼ cup freshly squeezed orange juice

1 tablespoon Dijon mustard

1 tablespoon Worcestershire sauce

2 garlic cloves, smashed

1 teaspoon kosher salt

1 teaspoon freshly ground black pepper

FOR THE SHISH KEBAB

1 pound tender steak, trimmed of fat and cut into 1-inch cubes

1 large green bell pepper, cut into chunks

1 large red onion, cut into chunks

8 ounces mushrooms, trimmed and cleaned

8 ounces cherry tomatoes

Nonstick cooking spray (optional)

10 metal skewers

Kosher salt

Freshly ground black pepper

TO MAKE THE MARINADE

1. Combine the oil, soy sauce, red wine vinegar, orange juice, mustard, Worcestershire sauce, garlic, salt, and pepper in a large resealable bag.

TO MAKE THE SHISH KEBAB

2. Add the steak, green bell pepper, onion, mushrooms, and tomatoes, seal the bag, and squish the contents around to combine and distribute the liquid. Transfer to the refrigerator for 4 hours or overnight.

3. Light a charcoal grill or heat a gas grill to medium-high heat (375°F). Alternatively, spray a grill pan with nonstick cooking spray and heat it on medium-high heat on the stovetop. Drain and discard the marinade. Thread the skewers, distributing evenly the meat, green bell pepper, onion, mushrooms, and tomatoes until all the skewers are full. Pat them dry using paper towels. Season with salt and pepper and sear on the grill over direct heat, about 3 minutes per side. Move skewers to a cooler part of the grill to finish cooking, about 3 minutes more.

4. Transfer to a plate and allow the meat to rest for 5 minutes before serving.

Braised Bulgogi Short Ribs

FREEZER-FRIENDLY · MAKE AHEAD · ONE POT

Grilled or panfried, bulgogi is amazing. The problem is, full-on Korean-inspired barbecue is time-consuming. This braised version gives you the best of both worlds: savory, sweet-salty meat and quick one-pot cleanup. Serve it garnished with toasted sesame seeds, thinly sliced scallions, and slivers of pear.

Serves 4

PREP TIME:
15 minutes

COOK TIME:
3 hours
15 minutes,
plus 5 minutes
to rest

1½ tablespoons
　extra-virgin olive oil
2 pounds boneless
　beef short ribs
½ teaspoon freshly
　ground black pepper
3 large carrots, peeled and
　sliced into 3-inch logs
3 medium garlic cloves, minced
1½ tablespoons fresh
　ginger, minced
½ cup rice wine (mirin) or sweet
　white wine, such as a Riesling

⅓ cup low-sodium soy sauce
¼ cup apple juice
2 teaspoons toasted sesame oil
½ cup plus 2 tablespoons
　water, divided
⅓ cup dark brown sugar, packed
2 tablespoons Chinese black
　vinegar or unseasoned
　rice vinegar
2 cups cooked white
　rice, for serving

1. Preheat the oven to 325°F.

2. In a Dutch oven over high heat on the stovetop, heat the oil until shimmering. Season the ribs with pepper and sear until the meat is browned on all sides, about 4 minutes per side. Transfer to a platter and reserve.

3. Reduce the heat to medium and add the carrots, cooking for 4 minutes, stirring occasionally. Add the garlic and ginger and continue cooking, stirring constantly, for 1 minute. Add the rice wine and scrape up any browned bits from the bottom of the pan. Simmer for 2 minutes before adding the soy sauce, apple juice, sesame oil, ½ cup of water, brown sugar, and black vinegar. Stir to combine.

4. Return the meat to the Dutch oven. Bring to a simmer and transfer to the oven. To keep the meat submerged, halfway through cooking, turn the beef once and add the remaining 2 tablespoons of water. When the meat is fork-tender after about 3 hours, remove from the oven and let rest for 5 minutes before serving with rice.

TROUBLESHOOTING TIP: If you find that your sauce is too thin, remove the meat and whisk 2 teaspoons of cornstarch into the liquid. Simmer the sauce until it is thickened, about 2 minutes.

German-Inspired Rouladen

This hearty, punchy dish originating in Germany has the makings of a great winter dinner. Although this version is braised in the oven, you can also cook the meat on the stovetop. Just cover and cook over low heat until tender, usually about 90 minutes.

PREP TIME:
30 minutes

COOK TIME:
2 hours

8 (¼-inch-thick) slices
  top-round beef
Kosher salt
Freshly ground black pepper
⅓ cup dark mustard, divided
8 bacon slices, cooked
  until lightly crispy
8 medium-sized dill pickles,
  sliced into spears
2 medium onions, finely
  chopped, divided

4 tablespoons unsalted butter
1 tablespoon extra-virgin
  olive oil
1 large carrot, chopped
1 large celery stalk, chopped
1 large garlic clove, minced
1 cup dry red wine,
  such as merlot
2 cups low-sodium beef broth
1 tablespoon cornstarch
¼ cup water

1. Preheat the oven to 325°F.

2. Gently pound the beef slices with a meat mallet until even and about ⅛-inch thick. Lay the meat out on a clean work surface and season with salt and pepper on both sides. Spread about 2 teaspoons of mustard on each slice. Place a strip of cooked bacon lengthwise on each slice, followed by a strip of pickle and 1½ teaspoons each of the chopped onions. Roll up the beef slices around the bacon, pickles, and onions, tucking in the sides and securing them with toothpicks or cooking twine.

3. In a large Dutch oven over medium-high heat on the stovetop, heat the butter and olive oil. Working in batches, sear the meat, about 3 minutes per side. Remove and reserve.

4. Reduce the heat to medium and add the remaining onions in a single, even layer. Let the onions cook without stirring them until they are soft and translucent, about 5 minutes. Add the carrot and celery and cook for 6 minutes more. Stir, scraping up browned bits from the bottom of the pan. Add the garlic and cook 1 minute before adding the red wine. Bring to a boil and simmer for 2 minutes before adding the broth.

5. Nestle the meat into the Dutch oven and return to a boil. Cover and transfer to the oven to cook for about 90 minutes, or until the meat is fork-tender.

6. Remove the meat and reserve. Strain the solids from sauce. Dissolve the cornstarch in water and slowly pour in the cornstarch mixture, stirring constantly until slightly thickened. Taste and adjust the seasonings, if needed.

7. Serve, topping the meat with the gravy.

PREP TIP: You can transfer everything to a slow cooker after adding a broth. Cook on low for 6 hours.

Beef Stroganoff Pot Roast

MAKE AHEAD · ONE POT

This old-timey classic is named after Count Pavel Aleksandrovich Stroganov, a member of a wealthy Russian family that allied itself with Ivan the Terrible. When it came to cuisine, Count Pavel had a taste for both French and Russian food, hence this delicious beef dish that keeps well in the refrigerator.

Serves 6

PREP TIME:
15 minutes

COOK TIME:
3 hours
40 minutes

1 (2-pound) beef chuck roast
½ teaspoon kosher salt, plus more to season
½ teaspoon freshly ground black pepper, plus more to season
1 tablespoon extra-virgin olive oil
1½ tablespoons unsalted butter
1 cup sliced baby portabella mushrooms
1 medium onion, finely chopped
3 garlic cloves, minced
⅓ cup brandy or bourbon whiskey

1 (10.5-ounce) can low-sodium beef broth
1 tablespoon Worcestershire sauce
1 tablespoon grainy mustard
1 teaspoon red wine vinegar or sherry
2 dried bay leaves
½ cup sour cream
1 (12-ounce) package egg noodles, cooked
1½ tablespoons minced fresh flat-leaf parsley, for garnish

1. Season the chuck roast generously with salt and pepper.

2. In a large Dutch oven over high heat on the stovetop, heat the oil until shimmering. Brown the meat for 3 to 5 minutes per side. Remove and reserve the meat.

3. Reduce the heat to medium and add the butter. When melted, add the mushrooms, stirring occasionally, for 4 minutes. Add the onion and continue cooking for 5 minutes before adding the garlic and cooking 1 minute more.

4. Add the brandy and bring to a boil. Simmer for 2 minutes, then return the beef to the Dutch oven, along with the broth, Worcestershire sauce, mustard, red wine vinegar, bay leaves, salt, and pepper. Return to a boil, cover, and transfer to the oven to cook until fork-tender, 2½ to 3 hours.

5. Remove from the oven. Transfer the meat to a large cutting board and shred it into hunks. Reserve the meat and discard the fat.

6. Remove and discard the bay leaves from the sauce. Whisk in the sour cream. Simmer over medium heat for 3 to 4 minutes to allow the sauce to thicken. Return the meat to the Dutch oven and warm through, about 5 to 10 minutes.

7. Serve atop the noodles, garnished with parsley.

PREP TIP: You can transfer the ingredients to a slow cooker once everything is added in step 3. Cook on low for 8 to 10 hours.

Lomo Saltado (Peruvian-Inspired Beef Stir-Fry)

ONE POT

When I traveled to Peru a few years ago, I was immediately struck by its fascinating cuisine, built from seemingly disparate ingredients. Iconic *lomo saltado* embodies that spirit: Its rich marinade is a mash-up of Eastern and Western flavors.

Serves 4

PREP TIME:
15 minutes, plus 4 hours to marinate

COOK TIME:
10 minutes, plus 2 minutes to rest

FOR THE MARINADE

4 garlic cloves, crushed

⅔ cup soy sauce

2 tablespoons red wine vinegar

2 teaspoons Worcestershire sauce

½ teaspoon dried oregano

½ teaspoon ground cumin

2 tablespoons water

½ teaspoon kosher salt

½ teaspoon freshly ground black pepper

1½ pounds filet mignon or strip steak, cubed and trimmed of fat

FOR THE LOMO SALTADO

1 tablespoon vegetable oil

1 large red onion, sliced into large slivers

2 tomatoes, halved, seeded, and cut into eighths

1 tablespoon aji amarillo paste or 1 jalapeño, minced

4 tablespoons pisco or tequila

½ (16-ounce) package frozen French fries, cooked until crisp

1½ cups finely chopped cilantro, for garnish

⅔ cup finely chopped fresh flat-leaf parsley, for garnish

2 cups cooked white rice, for serving

TO MAKE THE MARINADE

1. In a large, resealable bag, combine the garlic, soy sauce, red wine vinegar, Worcestershire sauce, oregano, cumin, water, salt, and pepper. Add the steak, seal the bag and squish the contents around to evenly distribute the marinade, and transfer to the refrigerator for at least 4 hours and up to overnight.

TO MAKE THE LOMO SALTADO

2. Drain the meat, reserving the marinade. Pat dry with paper towels.

3. In a large skillet or wok, heat the oil over high heat until shimmering. Cook the meat quickly, tossing it until it is browned on all sides, about 3 minutes. Remove the meat with a slotted spoon and reserve.

4. Reduce the heat to medium-high. Add the onion and cook for 1 minute before adding the tomatoes, aji amarillo paste, pisco, and reserved marinade. Cook for 3 minutes, adding the beef back in for the last 1 minute to warm. Remove from the heat and allow the meat to rest for 2 minutes.

5. Toss the meat and sauce with the fries, garnish with the cilantro and parsley, and serve with the rice.

> **SUBSTITUTION TIP**: You can find pisco at any well-stocked liquor store. Tequila is an acceptable, though not equivalent, substitute. Aji amarillo paste can be found at Latin markets or ordered online. Its flavor is singular, though you can use jalapeño in its place.

Portuguese-Inspired Beef Stew with Bacon and Onions

This smoky, oniony beef stew is a perfect cold weather restorative. I like to serve it atop mashed potatoes, but serving it over rice or egg noodles is a safe bet, too!

Serves 6

PREP TIME:
30 minutes

COOK TIME:
3 hours
plus
30 minutes
to rest

2½ pounds beef stew meat

1 teaspoon kosher salt, plus more to season

½ teaspoon freshly ground black pepper, plus more to season

½ pound thick-cut, hardwood-smoked bacon, chopped

2 tablespoons unsalted butter, divided

2 cups thinly sliced onions

10 garlic cloves, finely chopped

3 cups dry white wine, such as pinot grigio

1½ cups low-sodium beef broth, divided

2 tablespoons all-purpose flour

½ teaspoon ground allspice

¼ teaspoon red pepper flakes

2 dried bay leaves

3 tablespoons water, as needed

2 tablespoons finely chopped fresh flat-leaf parsley, for garnish

1. Preheat the oven to 350°F. Season the beef with salt and pepper and set aside.

2. In a large Dutch oven over medium-high heat on the stovetop, cook the bacon until it is crispy, about 7 minutes. Transfer the bacon to a paper-towel-lined plate to drain. Reserve 2 tablespoons of rendered fat, discarding the rest.

3. Add 1 tablespoon of butter to the Dutch oven. When melted, sear the beef in batches until it is nicely browned on all sides, about 7 minutes. Transfer to a large plate.

4. Lower the heat to medium and add the remaining 1 tablespoon of butter. When melted, add the onions, garlic, and white wine. Bring to a low boil and simmer for 3 minutes, scraping browned bits from the bottom of the pan. Add the broth and continue cooking until the onions are soft and translucent, about 7 minutes.

5. Return the bacon and beef to the Dutch oven and add the flour, all-spice, red pepper flakes, bay leaves, salt, and pepper. Stir, bring to a boil, cover and transfer to the oven to cook for 2 to 2½ hours, or until the meat is fork-tender. Add a few tablespoons of water halfway through if the liquid appears dry.

6. Remove the stew from the oven and let rest on the stovetop, covered, for 30 minutes. Taste and adjust seasoning, if needed.

7. Ladle into bowls and garnish with parsley.

PREP TIP: This recipe can easily be adapted for a slow cooker. Cook on low for 8 hours.

Texas Red Chili

FREEZER-FRIENDLY · MAKE AHEAD · ONE POT

Not all chili has beans, and some chili diehards consider beans sacrilege. Deeply nuanced, russet-hued, and spicy, this bowl of red chili gets its heat from ground ancho chili. I love it atop ½ cup of cooked elbow macaroni and garnished with crushed corn chips for crunch.

Serves 8

PREP TIME:
15 minutes

COOK TIME:
2 hours
35 minutes,
plus
10 minutes
to rest

3 pounds beef stew meat

½ tablespoon kosher salt, plus more to season

1 teaspoon freshly ground black pepper, plus more to season

1 teaspoon ground cumin

¼ cup ground ancho chili or ground chili powder

2 tablespoons masa harina

2½ cups water, divided

1 tablespoon vegetable oil

4 ounces pancetta or bacon, finely chopped

½ cup finely chopped onion

6 large garlic cloves, minced

2¼ cups low-sodium beef broth

1 tablespoon light brown sugar, packed

1½ tablespoons distilled white vinegar

½ cup sour cream

1 lime, cut into wedges

1. Season the meat with salt and pepper.

2. In a small bowl, combine the salt, pepper, cumin, ground chili, masa harina, and ¼ cup of water, stirring until it forms a smooth, loose paste.

3. In a large Dutch oven over medium-high heat on the stovetop, heat the oil until shimmering. Brown the meat in three batches on all sides, about 6 minutes per batch. Transfer to a large plate.

4. Reduce the heat to medium. Add the pancetta, onion, and ¼ cup of water. Cook, scraping up browned bits from the bottom of the pan and stirring occasionally until the onion is soft and translucent, about 7 minutes. Add the garlic and cook, stirring, for 1 minute more.

5. Return the meat to the Dutch oven and add the broth, remaining 2 cups of water, and reserved chili paste. Once again, scrape the browned bits from the bottom. Reduce the heat to low and cook, uncovered, for 2 hours or until the meat is fork-tender.

6. Add the brown sugar and white vinegar. Taste and adjust the seasoning, if needed. Raise the heat to medium and simmer, stirring occasionally, for 10 minutes.

7. Turn off the heat. Roughly shred the meat using two forks and let it rest for 10 minutes to absorb some of the liquid.

8. Serve with sour cream and lime wedges.

> **TIP:** Rather than cooking on low heat on the stove for 2 hours as described in step 4, you can transfer everything to the slow cooker. Cook on low for 8 to 10 hours. The chili can be made ahead, and you can freeze it in an airtight container for up to 3 months.

3

PORK

If you were stranded on a desert island and could choose just five foods to live on, what would yours be? Pork is one of mine. For starters, it's incredibly versatile. Depending on the cut, it's lean or lush. It can be succulent, smoky, or a combination of both. A great conductor for marinades, it's also a vehicle for sultry, slow-braised flavors. Frankly speaking, I can't imagine a world without forever-cooked pork shoulder, peppery bacon, and panfried chops. Can you?

←───◄◄ COCHINITA PIBIL WITH PICKLED RED ONIONS, PAGE 70

COMMON CUTS

When buying pork, look for meat with firm, pink flesh. Avoid damp, pale, or soft meat. It's best to seek out pasture-raised or organic pork (see page 4) if your budget allows. It'll result in tastier, richer dishes.

Back Ribs

Also referred to as baby back ribs, back ribs are cut from the blade and center portions of the loin. Smaller than spareribs, they're prized for the meat between the bones. Gussy them up with a dry rub or sauce and grill a 1½- to 2-pound rack over indirect, 325°F heat for 1½ to 2 hours per pound, or until tender.

Bacon

Bacon comes from the side portion—or belly—of the pig. It's cured and smoked to make bacon, which is sold either presliced or in a slab with a rind of fat that should be removed prior to slicing. Bacon can be panfried in an ungreased frying pan over medium heat and flipped so it browns and crisps evenly. Better yet, roast it on a foil-lined baking sheet at 375°F for 15 to 20 minutes, or until uniformly browned and crisp.

Ham

Cut from the rear leg, ham is typically cured, smoked, or processed somehow. It can be wet-cured or dry-cured, rubbed with salt and spices. A ½-inch, bone-in ham steak should be grilled for 6 minutes or until the internal temperature reaches 145°F. A fully cooked ham should be roasted at 350°F for 20 minutes per pound, or until an instant-read thermometer inserted into the center reads 145°F.

Pork Chops

A pork chop's name—be it porterhouse, rib eye, or sirloin—is determined by the area it comes from within the loin. The porterhouse is from the pork loin (loin end from the middle of the loin and back), with the bone and tenderloin intact. The rib eye is cut from the rib area of the loin, next to the blade chops, and the sirloin is a tougher cut, located on the loin to the hip. When braised, ¾-inch chops should be cooked over medium-high heat for 6 to 10 minutes, or until they are evenly browned. Then, add enough liquid to reach halfway up the sides of the pork. Return to a boil, cover, and simmer until tender. Alternatively, grill the chops over direct, medium heat for 8 to 12 minutes, turning once halfway through. Chops are done when an instant-read thermometer inserted into the center reads 145°F.

Pork Loin

Sold bone-in or deboned, the pork loin hails from between the pig's shoulder and the start of its leg. Ideal for brining, rubs, and barbecues, a 3- to 5-pound roast can be grilled over indirect, 325°F heat for 12 to 15 minutes per pound, or until tender. Meanwhile, a 4- to 5-pound roast should be cooked in a shallow pan at 350°F for 25 to 40 minutes per pound.

Pork Shoulder

Also called pork butt or Boston butt, pork shoulder—as you may have guessed— is cut from the pig's shoulder. Fairly tough and well marbled, a 3- to 4-pound shoulder can be grilled over indirect, 325°F heat for 40 to 75 minutes per pound, or until tender. A 3- to 6-pound shoulder can also be roasted at 275°F for 55 to 85 minutes, or until tender.

Pork Tenderloin

Long, thin, and lean, pork tenderloin—sometimes called pork fillet or gentleman's cut—comes from the area between the pig's shoulder and the beginning of its leg. It's an ideal choice for a small dinner party. Roast or grill it whole for a quick weeknight dinner at 325°F for 25 minutes per pound, or slice it into medallions like a loaf of French bread and sauté. Whatever you choose, it needs to reach an internal temperature of 145°F.

Sausage

Made from ground pork, pork sausage can be seasoned many ways. Generally greasy and richly flavored, it's most commonly seen as breakfast sausage, Italian sausage, bratwurst, or chorizo. It can also be smoked to produce Polish kielbasa or Cajun andouille.

Spareribs

Cut from the hog's belly, spareribs are larger and meatier than back ribs. They can be prepared with a dry rub or sauce. A 3½- to 4-pound rack should then be grilled over indirect, 325°F heat for 1½ to 2 hours, or until tender. It can also be roasted at 350°F for 1½ to 2 hours, or until tender.

WHAT COULD GO WRONG?

Q: Why is my pork always dried out?
The optimal internal cooking temperature for pork is 145°F. Allow cooked pork to rest for 10 to 20 minutes once it's removed from the heat. When you're checking the meat's temperature, make sure you avoid the bone. Bone runs much hotter, and touching it with your thermometer leads to an inaccurate reading.

Q: Does the color of cooked pork matter?
Pork is typically ideally cooked to a rosy medium, particularly for chops.

Q: What is the best way to thaw frozen pork?
Always thaw pork in the refrigerator in its wrapping. Generally speaking, a small roast takes 3 to 5 hours per pound to defrost, while a large roast takes 4 to 7 hours per pound. A 1-inch-thick chop requires 12 to 14 hours of thawing time. Ground pork's thaw time is determined by its package thickness.

Q: Can I cook a pork roast if it's not completely thawed?
It is safe to cook frozen or partially frozen pork in the oven, on the stove, or on the grill without thawing it first. Just know that the required cooking time is about 50 percent longer. However, do not cook frozen pork in a slow cooker. It will affect the timing; it's also unsafe since the meat doesn't come to the correct temperature quickly enough. Cook a frozen pork roast in the oven at 325°F until an instant-read thermometer inserted into the thickest part reads 145°F.

Q: How long can I keep my fresh pork in the refrigerator?

Sealed, prepackaged, fresh cuts of pork can be kept in the refrigerator for 2 to 4 days, while sealed ground pork will keep in the refrigerator for 1 to 2 days. If you do plan on keeping pork longer than 2 to 3 days prior to cooking it, wrap the meat well and store it in the freezer for up to 3 months. Bacon, smoked sausage, hot dogs, and lunchmeat can be kept refrigerated for up to 7 days. Leftover pork should be placed in the refrigerator within 2 hours of serving and kept for no more than 5 days. Well-wrapped leftovers can be kept in the freezer for up to 3 months.

Panfried Pork Chops with Pan Gravy

5 INGREDIENTS OR FEWER · 30 MINUTES OR LESS · ONE POT

A staple in many Filipino households, lightning-quick panfried pork chops are typically served with rice and a vinegar-laced tomato-onion salad. Go all out and shower the rice with fried garlic. Although you'll find it in most Asian markets, your best bet is to make your own to use as needed.

Serves 4

PREP TIME:
5 minutes

COOK TIME:
10 minutes

8 thinly sliced, center-cut boneless or bone-in pork chops
Kosher salt
Freshly ground black pepper

1 tablespoon vegetable oil
2 eggs, lightly beaten
½ cup water
2 cups cooked white rice, for serving

1. Season the pork chops with salt and pepper.

2. In a large skillet, heat the oil over medium-high heat until shimmering. Dip the meat in the eggs, shaking off any excess. Panfry until golden and cooked through, when an instant-read thermometer inserted into the meat registers 145°F, 2 to 3 minutes per side. Transfer to a platter and tent loosely with foil.

3. Pour the water into the pan and bring to a boil, scraping up the browned bits from the bottom of the pan. Drizzle this mixture over the meat and serve immediately with rice. If you'd like, add your favorite vegetable.

PREP TIP: For extra flavor, marinate the meat in a mixture of soy sauce, minced garlic, and calamansi juice overnight.

Oven-Baked Italian Sausage and Peppers

ONE POT

Typically, sausage and peppers are prepared on the stovetop, but I think that's awfully hands-on. Instead, this baked one-dish version takes care of itself: The meat cooks to an even, golden brown with no advance browning required.

Serves 6

PREP TIME:
15 minutes

COOK TIME:
35 minutes,
plus 5 minutes
to rest

6 Italian sausage links,
   hot or mild
1 green bell pepper, stemmed,
   seeded, and cut into
   ½-inch thick slices
1 red bell pepper, stemmed,
   seeded, and cut into
   ½-inch thick slices

1 large onion, cut into
   ½-inch thick slices
1 tablespoon extra-virgin
   olive oil
½ tablespoon balsamic vinegar
Kosher salt
Freshly ground black pepper

1. Adjust the oven rack to the lower-middle position and preheat the oven to 375°F.

2. Arrange the sausage, bell peppers, and onion in a 9-by-13-inch baking sheet. Drizzle with the olive oil and balsamic vinegar. Season with salt and pepper and transfer to the oven to bake for 30 to 35 minutes, or until golden brown and cooked through.

3. Remove from the oven and let rest for 5 minutes before serving.

> **TROUBLESHOOTING TIP:** Cooking time depends entirely on your oven. If you haven't achieved a golden-brown color within 30 minutes, continue cooking, but check on it in 5-minute increments. If there's any pink, or if the juices that run out are bloody or pink and not clear, the sausage needs more cooking time.

Pork Tonkatsu

A Japanese-inspired take on breaded, panfried pork, these cutlets benefit from extra-crunchy panko bread crumbs and a final spurt of lemon. Serve yours with katsu sauce, which you'll find in the Asian aisle of most well-stocked grocery stores.

PREP TIME:
5 minutes,
plus
15 minutes
to chill

COOK TIME:
10 minutes

4 (5-ounce) pork cutlets,
 ½-inch thick
Kosher salt
Freshly ground black pepper
1 cup all-purpose flour

2 large eggs
2 cups panko bread crumbs
1 tablespoon vegetable oil
½ lemon, cut into wedges
Katsu sauce

1. Place the meat in a single layer between two sheets of plastic wrap and, using a meat mallet or rolling pin, pound the cutlets to ¼-inch thick. Season both sides of the meat with salt and pepper.

2. Gather three small, shallow bowls. In the first, pour in the flour and season with salt and pepper. In the second, whisk the eggs with a fork. In the third, pour in the bread crumbs and season with salt and pepper.

3. Lightly coat each cutlet in the flour, then in the egg, and finally in the bread crumbs, pressing the bread crumbs onto the pork for an even coat. Place them on a baking sheet and transfer to the refrigerator for 15 minutes to help the breading adhere.

4. In a large skillet over medium-high heat, heat the oil until shimmering. Add the cutlets to the pan and cook until golden, about 3 minutes per side. Transfer to paper towels to drain. Lightly season with salt and serve with lemon and katsu sauce.

INGREDIENT TIP: Get an extra-good crisp by double-frying the cutlets before serving. Just panfry, drain, and panfry again.

Spice-Rubbed, Slow-Roasted Pork Shoulder

FREEZER-FRIENDLY · MAKE AHEAD · ONE POT

This recipe calls for an aromatic herb and spice rub, which is slathered on the pork before it's cooked ultra–low and slow. It yields meltingly delicious meat that can be tucked into tacos or sandwiches or served alongside mashed potatoes or rice. Leftovers can be frozen in an airtight container for up to 3 months.

Serves 12

PREP TIME:
5 minutes

COOK TIME:
8 hours, plus 15 minutes to rest

2 teaspoons ground cumin
1 teaspoon garlic powder
1 teaspoon onion powder
1 teaspoon dried oregano
1 teaspoon dried thyme
½ teaspoon ground cinnamon
½ teaspoon ground allspice

1 tablespoon kosher salt
1 teaspoon freshly ground black pepper
2 tablespoons extra-virgin olive oil
5- to 6-pound boneless pork shoulder

1. Adjust oven rack to middle position and preheat the oven to 275°F.

2. In a small bowl, combine the cumin, garlic powder, onion powder, oregano, thyme, cinnamon, allspice, salt, pepper, and olive oil.

3. Place the pork in a large roasting pan and slather it all over with the rub. Transfer to the oven to cook for 7 to 8 hours, or until it is meltingly tender with a caramelized exterior.

4. Transfer to a cutting board and let rest for 15 minutes. Roughly shred the meat, discarding fatty bits. Serve.

SUBSTITUTION TIP: Feel free to replace the rub with your favorite homemade or store-bought spice blend.

Meaty Sunday Gravy

ONE POT · MAKE AHEAD · FREEZER-FRIENDLY

Make a double batch of this delicious meal, then use it to top garlic bread. Sprinkle it with some mozzarella, Parmesan, and a shower of garlic powder and bake it in a preheated 375°F oven until the cheese is melted and bubbly. Spaghetti sandwich!

Serves 6

PREP TIME:
20 minutes

COOK TIME:
1 hour

1 tablespoon extra-virgin
  olive oil
1½ pounds hot or mild Italian
  sausage, casings removed
4 ounces diced pancetta
1 large carrot, finely chopped
1 large onion, finely chopped
2 celery stalks, trimmed
  and finely chopped
3 garlic cloves, minced
3 ounces dried mushrooms,
  such as cremini, reconstituted
  in ½ cup hot water
½ cup dry red wine,
  such as Chianti

¾ cup low-sodium beef broth
1 (28-ounce) can
  crushed tomatoes
4 tablespoons unsalted butter
1 teaspoon kosher salt
½ teaspoon freshly
  ground black pepper
¼ teaspoon ground nutmeg
2 dried bay leaves
2 Parmesan rinds (optional),
  plus ½ cup grated Parmesan
1 pound dried spaghetti,
  cooked al dente

1. In a large Dutch oven, heat the oil over medium-high heat until shimmering. Add the sausage, breaking it into small bits and cooking through until nicely browned, about 7 minutes.

2. Nudge the meat to the side of the pan. Reduce the heat to medium and add the pancetta. Brown, stirring often, until golden, about 5 minutes. Add the carrot, onion, and celery and continue cooking for 6 minutes until the vegetables are just beginning to soften. Add the garlic and cook 1 minute more.

3. Drain the mushrooms, straining the liquid and adding it back to the Dutch oven. Finely chop the mushrooms and add them to the pan along with the red wine. Simmer for 3 minutes and stir all ingredients including the meat together. Add the broth, tomatoes, butter, salt, pepper, nutmeg, bay leaves, and Parmesan rinds (if using). Reduce the heat to low, loosely cover, and simmer, stirring occasionally, for 30 minutes.

4. Discard the bay leaves and cheese rinds. Taste and adjust the seasoning, if needed. Serve atop the spaghetti adding the grated Parmesan on top.

INGREDIENT TIP: Although canned San Marzano tomatoes are more expensive, using them makes all the difference in the world. If they're peeled and whole, zap them in a blender to puree and proceed with the recipe as directed. You can substitute fresh white button mushrooms or baby portabella mushrooms for dried mushrooms, but the flavor will not be as rich.

Cochinita Pibil with Pickled Red Onions

If you have access to fresh or frozen banana leaves, snap them up. Then, unfold two leaves (thaw first if using frozen ones), laying them crosswise in your roasting pan and removing any excess leaves (you'll likely need to trim them). Enclose the slathered pork inside. This lends a subtle, sweet aroma to the meat. Note to banana leaf novices: Do not eat the leaves.

 Serves 12

PREP TIME:
15 minutes, plus 1 hour to pickle

COOK TIME:
5 hours, plus 10 minutes to rest

FOR THE PORK

½ (3.5-ounce) package achiote paste

1 teaspoon ground cumin

1½ teaspoons kosher salt

1 teaspoon freshly ground black pepper

½ cup freshly squeezed orange juice

1 cup freshly squeezed lime juice

1 (6-pound) boneless pork shoulder

1 large white onion, trimmed and cut into ¼-inch thick slices

FOR THE ONIONS

3 red onions, trimmed and thinly sliced

½ teaspoon dried Mexican oregano

½ teaspoon sugar

½ cup apple cider vinegar

½ teaspoon kosher salt

¼ cup water

½ cup cilantro leaves, finely chopped

2 (10.84-ounce, 10-count) packages of corn tortillas

2 limes, cut into wedges

TO MAKE THE PORK

1. Adjust the oven rack to the lower-middle position and preheat the oven to 325°F.

2. In a small bowl, combine the achiote paste, cumin, salt, pepper, orange juice, and lime juice. Mash with a fork to make a smooth, loose paste.

3. Place the meat in a roasting pan and rub it all over with the seasoning paste. Scatter with the onion slices and cover with foil. Transfer to the oven to cook for 4 or 5 hours, periodically basting with pan juices after 2 hours.

TO MAKE THE ONIONS

4. Meanwhile, in a medium airtight container, place the red onions. Add the oregano, sugar, apple cider vinegar, salt, and water. Seal the container, shake to combine, and transfer to the refrigerator to pickle for at least 1 hour but up to 1 week.

5. When the pork is fall-apart tender, remove it from the oven. Transfer it to a large cutting board and let it rest for 10 minutes. Shred the meat, discarding the fat. Serve with the cilantro, tortillas, lime wedges, and reserved pickled red onions.

PREP TIP: If you're fortunate enough to live near a good Latin market, look for sour orange juice, which is made from bitter Seville oranges. Swap out the lime and orange juices for 1½ cups sour orange juice.

Cheesy Cilantro Pesto Pork Tenderloin

Featuring a bright, bold cilantro pesto and pepper Jack filling, this easy week-night pork tenderloin recipe can be prepared 1 day in advance and refrigerated until you're ready to cook it.

Serves 6

PREP TIME:
10 minutes

COOK TIME:
35 minutes,
plus
10 minutes
to rest

FOR THE PESTO

½ cup cilantro leaves

⅛ cup fresh flat-leaf parsley leaves, lightly packed

2 medium garlic cloves, chopped, divided

2 tablespoons walnuts, lightly toasted

⅛ cup grated Parmesan cheese

¼ teaspoon kosher salt

¼ teaspoon freshly ground black pepper

1 tablespoon freshly squeezed lemon juice

½ tablespoon water

¼ cup extra-virgin olive oil

FOR THE PORK

2 (1-pound) pork tenderloins, fat trimmed and sliced open lengthwise like books

½ cup shredded pepper Jack or Monterey Jack cheese

Kosher salt

Freshly ground black pepper

½ tablespoon extra-virgin olive oil

TO MAKE THE PESTO

1. Adjust the oven rack to the lower-middle position and preheat the oven to 375°F.

2. In a food processor fitted with a metal blade, pulse the cilantro, parsley, and garlic until a coarse paste is formed. With the food processor running, add the walnuts, Parmesan, salt, pepper, lemon juice, and water. Slowly drizzle in the olive oil. Process until smooth, stopping to scrape the pesto from the sides. Taste and adjust the seasonings, if needed. If you don't have a food processor, use a blender, working in small batches.

TO MAKE THE PORK

3. Place each tenderloin between two sheets of plastic wrap and, using a meat mallet or rolling pin, pound them to a ½-inch thickness.

4. Spread equal amounts of the pesto on one side of each tenderloin and top with the cheese. Roll up the meat and secure at ½-inch intervals with kitchen twine. Season with salt and pepper, place in the roasting pan with the seam sides up, and drizzle with the oil.

5. Transfer to the oven and cook until the pork reaches an internal temperature of 145°F, about 35 minutes. Remove the pork from the oven, tent with foil, and allow to rest for 10 minutes. Slice and serve.

PREP TIP: Tying a roast ensures its size is uniform for even cooking. It also prevents stuffing from spilling out. Don't skip the twine!

Massive Meatballs and Spaghetti

FREEZER-FRIENDLY · MAKE AHEAD

Spaghetti and meatballs is a cozy, feel-good meal, and the meatballs lend themselves to freezing. Try serving this dish with a dollop of whole-milk ricotta cheese for added richness.

Serves 4

PREP TIME:
10 minutes

COOK TIME:
40 minutes

FOR THE MEATBALLS

3 tablespoons extra-virgin olive oil, divided

1 cup whole milk

2¾ cups plain bread crumbs

1 pound ground pork

1 pound ground chuck

1 cup finely chopped fresh flat-leaf parsley

1 teaspoon dried basil

½ cup grated Parmesan

2 garlic cloves, grated

½ teaspoon red pepper flakes

1 teaspoon kosher salt

2 large eggs, lightly beaten

FOR THE SAUCE

2 tablespoons extra-virgin olive oil

4 garlic cloves, minced

1 (28-ounce) can crushed tomatoes with their juices

½ cup low-sodium beef broth

4 fresh basil leaves, stems attached

½ cup water

1 teaspoon kosher salt

½ teaspoon freshly ground black pepper

1 pound dried spaghetti, cooked al dente

TO MAKE THE MEATBALLS

1. Preheat the oven to 400°F and brush an 18-by-13-inch baking sheet with 1 tablespoon olive oil.

2. In a small bowl, combine the milk and bread crumbs and set aside.

3. In a large bowl, mix by hand until just combined the pork, beef, parsley, basil, Parmesan, garlic, red pepper flakes, salt, and eggs. Add the reserved bread crumb mixture and mix again until just combined.

4. With damp hands, shape the meat into four large balls. Place on the prepared baking sheet and transfer to the oven to bake for 25 to 30 minutes or until an instant-read thermometer inserted into the centers of each of the meatball registers 165°F.

TO MAKE THE SAUCE

5. While the meatballs are cooking, in a large saucepan over medium heat, heat the oil. Sauté the garlic, stirring constantly, until soft and fragrant, about 3 minutes. Add the tomatoes, broth, basil, water, salt, and pepper. Bring to a boil. Reduce the heat to low and simmer until thickened, about 30 minutes.

6. Remove the meatballs from the oven and mix into the sauce. Cover and continue cooking for 10 minutes or until the meatballs are cooked through.

7. Discard the basil leaves. Taste and adjust the seasonings, if needed. Serve atop spaghetti.

INGREDIENT TIP: Feel free to use your own combination of ground beef, pork, and veal, as long as it totals 2 pounds of meat.

Smothered Pork Chops

ONE POT

A Southern classic, smothered pork chops deserve to be in regular rotation on your dinner table. Equally doable as a weeknight meal or a special weekend treat, this crowd-pleaser is easy, hearty, and downright homey.

Serves 4

PREP TIME:
15 minutes

COOK TIME:
35 minutes,
plus 5 minutes
to rest

½ teaspoon ground
cayenne red pepper
½ teaspoon onion powder
½ teaspoon garlic powder
½ teaspoon kosher salt,
plus more to season
½ teaspoon freshly
ground black pepper,
plus more to season
4 (1½-inch-thick) pork
chops, bone-in preferred

1 tablespoon unsalted butter
1 tablespoon vegetable oil
1 large onion, thinly sliced
4 medium garlic cloves, minced
1½ tablespoons
all-purpose flour
2 fresh thyme sprigs
1½ cups low-sodium
chicken broth
½ cup buttermilk

1. In a small bowl, combine the cayenne pepper, onion powder, garlic powder, salt, and pepper. Season both sides of the pork chops with this mixture.

2. In a large cast-iron or nonstick skillet over medium-high heat, heat the butter and oil until the butter is melted. Panfry the pork chops to a golden brown, about 5 minutes per side. Transfer to a platter and tent with foil.

3. Add the onion to the skillet and cook until it is soft and translucent, about 7 minutes, scraping up browned bits from the bottom of the pan as the onion cooks. Reduce the heat to medium, add the garlic, and cook for 30 seconds until fragrant. Season with salt and pepper, sprinkle the flour on top, and cook, stirring constantly, for 1 minute. Reduce the heat to low and add the thyme sprigs, broth, and buttermilk.

4. Return the pork chops and any juices to the skillet. Simmer for 10 to 15 minutes or until an instant-read thermometer inserted into the center of the chops registers 145°F. Discard the thyme and taste. Adjust the seasoning, if needed. Remove from the heat and let rest for 5 minutes before serving.

Hawaiian-Inspired
Kalua Pulled Pork

5 INGREDIENTS OR FEWER · MAKE AHEAD · ONE POT

Although traditionally cooked in an underground oven, this version of the Hawaiian staple is home-kitchen–friendly. To speed up the process, cook it at 350°F for about 4 hours, taking care to add water to the roasting pan as needed to prevent burning.

Serves 10

PREP TIME:
5 minutes

COOK TIME:
7 hours

1 (5- to 6-pound) pork butt
1 tablespoon kosher salt
½ tablespoon liquid smoke
2 tablespoons soy sauce

3 to 4 cups water
1 (12-count) package
  Hawaiian sweet rolls,
  such as King's Hawaiian

1. Preheat the oven to 275°F.

2. Place the pork in a roasting pan. Using a small knife, score the meat all over to create a diamond pattern. Rub the salt, liquid smoke, and soy sauce onto the meat, taking care to get them into the cracks. Cover with foil and transfer to the oven to cook for 6 or 7 hours, until fork-tender. If the liquid level in the roasting pan gets low, add additional water.

3. Remove from the oven, uncover, and let cool enough to be able to handle.

4. Shred the pork, mix it with the pan sauce, and serve tucked into the Hawaiian rolls.

> **INGREDIENT TIP**: For even better results, line the roasting pan with banana leaves, enclosing the pork in them. Cover the pan with foil and proceed, discarding the banana leaves before serving.

Greek-Inspired Drunken Pork Stew

FREEZER-FRIENDLY · MAKE AHEAD · ONE POT

This is a wine-spiked, one-pot wonder full of bold flavor. Yet it takes almost no time to prepare since most of the magic happens during a slow-and-low braise. It can also finish in a slow cooker set on low for 8 hours.

PREP TIME:
15 minutes

COOK TIME:
4 hours
30 minutes,
plus 5 minutes
to rest

- 1½ pounds boneless pork shoulder, cut into 1-inch chunks
- 1 teaspoon kosher salt, plus more to season
- 1 teaspoon freshly ground black pepper, plus more to season
- 1 tablespoon Dijon mustard
- 2 tablespoons extra-virgin olive oil
- 1 medium onion, diced
- 1 Cubanelle pepper or sweet banana pepper, cored, seeded, and sliced into rings
- 3 garlic cloves, minced
- 1 cup dry red wine, such as cabernet sauvignon
- 8 ounces canned crushed tomatoes with their juices
- 1 teaspoon smoked paprika
- ½ teaspoon ground cayenne red pepper
- 1 teaspoon dried oregano
- ¼ teaspoon ground allspice
- 2 dried bay leaves
- 2 cups cooked rice or orzo, for serving

1. Adjust the oven rack to the lower-middle position and preheat the oven to 275°F.

2. In a medium bowl, season the meat generously with salt and pepper and toss with the mustard.

3. In a large Dutch oven over medium-high heat on the stovetop, heat the oil until it is shimmering. Working in batches, add the meat and sear it on all sides until it is well browned, about 8 minutes per batch.

4. When the meat is nearly finished browning, reduce the heat to medium and push the meat off to the side of the pan. Add the onion, pepper, and garlic to the Dutch oven. Sauté until the vegetables become soft and translucent, about 7 minutes.

5. Add the red wine, raise the heat to medium-high, and bring to a boil. Simmer for 3 minutes, stirring to scrape the browned bits from the bottom of the pan. Add the tomatoes, paprika, cayenne pepper, oregano, allspice, bay leaves, salt, and pepper. Stir to combine.

6. Return to a boil. Then, cover and transfer to the oven to cook until fork-tender, about 4 hours. Remove from the oven and discard the bay leaves. Allow to rest for 5 minutes, and serve with the rice.

INGREDIENT TIP: To brighten the dish, shower it with some fresh finely chopped dill before serving.

Pork Goulash

MAKE AHEAD • ONE POT

Hearty, heady, and russet-hued, this Hungarian staple can be served with boiled potatoes or atop egg noodles, as it is here. Pair it with a crisp, pickled cucumber salad loaded with freshly chopped dill.

PREP TIME:
20 minutes

COOK TIME:
2 hours

5 bacon slices, chopped

3 pounds boneless pork shoulder, cut into 1-inch chunks

1 teaspoon kosher salt, plus more to season

½ teaspoon freshly ground black pepper, plus more to season

1 tablespoon unsalted butter

1 large onion, chopped

2 red bell peppers, chopped

2 carrots, cut into coins

5 garlic cloves, minced

2 tablespoons paprika

¼ teaspoon ground caraway seeds

1 cup low-sodium chicken broth

3 tablespoons red wine vinegar

1 tablespoon Worcestershire sauce

¼ cup tomato paste

2 fresh thyme sprigs

1 pound egg noodles, cooked

Sour cream, for garnish

1. In a large, deep skillet, cook the bacon over medium-high heat until evenly browned, about 10 minutes. Remove the bacon with a slotted spoon and place it on a paper-towel-lined plate to drain. Reserve the drippings.

2. Season the pork liberally with salt and pepper. Working in batches, add the pork to the skillet and brown all over, about 6 minutes per batch. Remove the pork from the skillet and reserve.

3. Add the butter and let it melt before adding the onion, bell peppers, and carrots. Cook, stirring occasionally, for about 5 minutes, until the mixture is starting to foam.

4. Reduce the heat to medium and add the garlic, paprika, and caraway. Cook for 1 minute more. Add the broth, red wine vinegar, Worcestershire sauce, tomato paste, thyme sprigs, salt, and pepper. Return the pork and bacon to the skillet. Stir to combine.

5. Reduce the heat to low, cover, and braise on the stovetop for about 1½ hours, or until the meat is tender. Discard the thyme sprigs and remove and shred the meat, discarding fatty bits. Taste and season with additional salt and pepper, if needed.

6. Serve on top of egg noodles, garnished with a dollop of sour cream.

PREP TIP: This recipe can be finished in your slow cooker once all the ingredients (other than noodles and sour cream) are added. Cook on low for 6 to 8 hours.

Skewered Grilled Pork Souvlaki

MAKE AHEAD

This popular Greek street food is a fun skewered meat. You can eat it straight from the stick as suggested in this recipe, or take it off and serve with rice and a simple salad. Make it ahead and keep it in the refrigerator for an easy and filling weekday lunch.

Serves 4 to 6

PREP TIME:
10 minutes, plus 4 hours to marinate

COOK TIME:
10 minutes, plus 5 minutes to rest

1½ pounds pork tenderloin, cut into 1-inch cubes

1 large onion, cut into ¾-inch-thick wedges

¼ cup freshly squeezed lemon juice

¼ cup extra-virgin olive oil

4 garlic cloves, smashed

1 tablespoon dried oregano

¼ teaspoon salt

¼ teaspoon pepper

8 wood skewers, soaked in water for 20 minutes

Nonstick cooking spray (optional)

6 Greek pitas, warmed

¾ cup prepared tzatziki

1. In a large, resealable plastic bag, combine the pork, onion, lemon juice, olive oil, garlic, oregano, salt, and pepper. Seal the bag and transfer it to the refrigerator to marinate for 4 hours.

2. Drain and discard the marinade and pat the meat dry with a paper towel. On the skewers, alternate placing a piece of meat and a piece of onion, distributing evenly.

3. Light a charcoal grill or heat a gas grill on medium-high (375°F). Alternatively, spray a grill pan with nonstick cooking spray and heat on the stove over medium-high heat. Cook the skewered meat and onions, turning occasionally, until the pork is cooked through and the onions are tender, about 10 minutes.

4. Transfer to a platter and let the skewers rest for 5 minutes. Serve with the pita and drizzle with the tzatziki.

> **INGREDIENT TIP:** Make your own tzatziki by combining 2 cups of Greek yogurt, ½ cup of grated English or hothouse cucumbers (excess water squeezed out), 2 minced garlic cloves, 1½ tablespoons of chopped fresh dill, 2 teaspoons of lemon juice, and 1 tablespoon of olive oil. Season with salt and pepper.

Grilled Mojo-Marinated Butterfly Pork Chops

FREEZER-FRIENDLY · MAKE AHEAD

Convenient and loaded with citrusy flavor, these pork chops can be marinated and refrigerated up to 2 days in advance of cooking or frozen in a resealable bag with the marinade for up to 3 months.

Serves 4

PREP TIME:
10 minutes,
plus 1 hour to
marinate

COOK TIME:
15 minutes,
plus 5 minutes
to rest

4 butterfly or center-cut pork chops, 1½-inch thick
Juice of 1 lime
Juice of 1 orange
⅓ cup extra-virgin olive oil
4 medium garlic cloves, minced
1 teaspoon ground cumin
¼ cup chopped fresh cilantro leaves

1 teaspoon kosher salt, plus more to season
½ teaspoon freshly ground black pepper, plus more to season
Nonstick cooking spray (optional)

1. Place the pork in a resealable bag and add the lime juice, orange juice, olive oil, garlic, cumin, cilantro, salt, and pepper. Seal the bag and squish the contents around to combine. Place in the refrigerator to marinate at least 1 hour and up to 2 days.

2. Light a charcoal grill or heat a gas grill on medium-high (375°F). Alternatively, spray a grill pan with nonstick cooking spray and heat on the stove over medium-high heat.

3. Remove the pork from the refrigerator. Discard the marinade. Pat the meat dry with paper towels. Season with salt and pepper. Place on the hot grill and cook until well browned, 3 to 5 minutes per side. Move to a cooler part of the grill. Continue cooking until an instant-read thermometer inserted into thickest part of chop registers 145°F.

4. Remove and transfer to a platter to rest 5 minutes before serving.

INGREDIENT TIP: To complete the meal, serve the pork chops with rice, sautéed onions, and a pot of beans. Consider doubling and reserving half of the marinade so you can serve it alongside the cooked pork.

Savory Orange-Sage Baked Ham

MAKE AHEAD

Who says a baked ham has to be covered in a saccharine glaze? This version has tang and aromatics! Try panfrying the leftovers and tucking the ham into a toasted English muffin along with egg and cheese. You can also use the bone and some meat to make velvety split pea soup.

Serves 8 to 10

PREP TIME:
15 minutes

COOK TIME:
4 hours, plus 10 minutes to rest

1 (8- to 10-pound) smoked, bone-in ham
Kosher salt
Freshly ground black pepper
2½ tablespoons extra-virgin olive oil
1 bunch fresh sage leaves, chopped
2 tablespoons fresh thyme leaves, stemmed
1 stick unsalted butter, cut into chunks

1½ cups freshly squeezed orange juice
1 medium orange, cut into thin slices
¾ cup water
½ cup light brown sugar, packed
1 shallot, minced
¼ teaspoon allspice
1 cinnamon stick
1 pound baby carrots
1 large onion, trimmed and sliced

1. Adjust the oven rack to the lower-middle position and preheat the oven to 300°F. In a large roasting pan, use a small knife to score the ham all over to create a diamond pattern half-inch deep. Season with salt and pepper.

2. In a small bowl, mash together the olive oil, sage, and thyme to form a paste. Rub it onto the ham, taking care to get the paste into the cuts. Transfer the ham to the oven to cook for 3 hours.

3. While the ham is cooking, in a medium saucepan over medium heat, heat the butter, orange juice, orange slices, water, brown sugar, shallot, allspice, and cinnamon stick. Bring to a boil. Reduce the heat to low and simmer until the liquid is reduced and syrupy, about 35 minutes. Reserve this glaze.

4. After 3 hours, remove the ham from the oven. Skim the fat from the pan. Scatter the carrots and onion slices around the ham and pour the glaze on top of everything. Return the ham to the oven to continue cooking for 1 more hour, basting every 15 minutes, until the ham is caramelized and the skin is crispy.

5. Remove the meat from the oven and transfer to a cutting board to rest for 10 minutes. Carve and serve with the glaze and the carrots and onion slices.

Slow-Cooked, Oven-Baked Ribs

ONE POT

Grilling doesn't have to be a summer activity, but it can be a drag to grill in cold weather. Fortunately, these oven-baked ribs more than suffice as an alternative. Master the approach and then feel free to customize with your favorite seasonings and sauces.

Serves 4

PREP TIME:
10 minutes

COOK TIME:
4 hours
20 minutes,
plus 5 minutes
to rest

FOR THE RIBS

½ teaspoon all-purpose seasoning, such as Lawry's

½ teaspoon kosher salt

2 teaspoons freshly ground black pepper

1½ teaspoons onion powder

1 tablespoon ground chili powder, such as ancho

½ cup light brown sugar, packed

2 racks baby back ribs

1 cup apple juice, such as Mott's

1 cup grape juice, such as Welch's

FOR THE GLAZE

½ cup honey

½ cup barbecue sauce

1½ tablespoons Asian chili sauce, such as sriracha

¼ cup light brown sugar, packed

TO MAKE THE RIBS

1. Adjust the oven rack to the middle position and preheat the oven to 275°F. Line an 18-by-13-inch baking sheet with foil.

2. In a small bowl, combine the all-purpose seasoning, salt, pepper, onion powder, chili powder, and brown sugar.

3. Place the ribs on the prepared baking sheet and coat thoroughly with the rub. Transfer the meat to the oven to cook until the fat begins to liquidify or render, about 2 hours.

4. Lay out two 12-by-24-inch sheets of heavy-duty foil on the countertop and fold their edges tightly together to form one large sheet.

5. Remove the ribs from the oven and set them on top of the two connected sheets of foil. Return the ribs with the connected foil underneath them to the lined baking sheet. Pour the apple juice and grape juice on top of the ribs, then fold up the new foil, sealing it tightly so steam cannot escape. Return to the oven and continue cooking until the ribs are completely tender, about 1½ to 2 hours longer.

TO MAKE THE GLAZE

6. While the ribs are cooking, in a small bowl, mix the honey, barbecue sauce, chili sauce, and brown sugar.

7. Remove the ribs from the oven and raise the oven temperature to 375°F. Remove the ribs from sealed foil. Discard the liquid and return the ribs to the lined baking sheet, brushing them generously with the glaze. Return the ribs to the oven to cook until the glaze is burnished and sticky, 15 to 20 minutes. Remove from the oven and allow the ribs to sit for 5 minutes before serving.

Panfried Pork Schnitzel

30 MINUTES OR LESS

One of life's simple pleasures, Austrian schnitzel is ideally served with a side of spaetzle or boiled, buttery parsley potatoes. If you wish, pork can be swapped for veal (wiener schnitzel) or chicken (hänchen schnitzel).

PREP TIME:
5 minutes, plus 15 minutes to chill

COOK TIME:
10 minutes

4 pork cutlets, boneless, ½-inch thick

¼ cup all-purpose flour

½ teaspoon all-purpose seasoning, such as Lawry's

1 teaspoon garlic salt

1 teaspoon freshly ground black pepper, divided

2 large eggs

4 cups plain bread crumbs

1 teaspoon paprika

1 teaspoon kosher salt

1 tablespoon unsalted butter

2 tablespoons vegetable oil

½ lemon, cut into wedges

1. Place the cutlets in a single layer between two sheets of wax paper and, using a meat mallet or rolling pin, pound until ¼-inch thick.

2. Get three medium shallow bowls. In the first, combine the flour, all-purpose seasoning, garlic salt, and ½ teaspoon of pepper. In the second, whisk the eggs with a fork. In the third, combine the bread crumbs, paprika, salt, and remaining ½ teaspoon of pepper.

3. Lightly coat each cutlet in the flour, then in the egg, and finally in the bread crumbs, pressing the bread crumbs onto the pork for an even coat. Put them on an 18-by-13-inch baking sheet to transfer to the refrigerator for 15 minutes to help the breading adhere.

4. In a large skillet over medium-high heat, heat the butter and oil until hot. Add the cutlets to the skillet and cook until golden, about 3 minutes per side. Transfer to paper towels to drain. Lightly season with salt and serve with a lemon wedge.

> **INGREDIENT TIP:** For a quick pan sauce, mix ½ teaspoon salt, ½ tablespoon chopped fresh dill, and ½ cup full-fat sour cream in a small bowl. In a separate bowl, whisk together ¾ cup chicken broth and 1 tablespoon flour. After the cutlets are removed, pour the chicken broth mixture into the skillet over medium heat and scrape the browned bits off the bottom. Whisk ¼ cup of the hot chicken broth into the sour cream mixture. Pour into the skillet and simmer until slightly thickened. Do not let it boil.

Pork-Chive Dumplings

They're a little labor-intensive, but dumplings are a reliable, bite-sized way to appeal to a crowd. Trot them out as an appetizer at a small party or make a huge batch for a weekend meal with family or friends.

PREP TIME:
30 minutes,
plus 1 hour to
chill

COOK TIME:
35 minutes

FOR THE DUMPLINGS

1¼ pounds ground pork

1 large egg, beaten

1 tablespoon grated fresh ginger

½ teaspoon kosher salt

¼ teaspoon freshly
ground black pepper

⅓ cup finely chopped
fresh chives

2 tablespoons cornstarch

1 package round
wonton wrappers

FOR THE DIPPING SAUCE

2 tablespoons Chinese black
vinegar or rice vinegar

¼ cup soy sauce

1 teaspoon sesame oil

1 teaspoon hot chili oil

TO MAKE THE DUMPLINGS

1. In a medium bowl, mix together the pork, egg, ginger, salt, pepper, and chives. Transfer to the refrigerator for 1 hour to let the flavors meld.

2. Bring a large pot of water to a rolling boil. Sprinkle a clean work surface or a 9-by-13-inch baking sheet with cornstarch to keep the dumplings from sticking. Add 1 tablespoon of filling to the center of each wonton wrapper. Fold each one into a half-moon shape. Dip your finger in water and moisten the edge of the wrapper, pressing edges together to seal.

3. Boil a large pot of water over medium-high heat. Working in batches, carefully drop the dumplings into the water. Return the water to a boil and cook for 5 to 8 minutes, per batch, or until the dumplings float to the top and the filling is cooked through.

TO MAKE THE DIPPING SAUCE

4. While the dumpling mixture is chilling, in a small bowl, combine the black vinegar, soy sauce, sesame oil, and chili oil. Reserve.

5. Carefully remove the dumplings with a slotted spoon and transfer to a serving plate. Serve with the dipping sauce.

Vietnamese-Inspired Caramel Pork

This iconic Vietnamese entrée toes the line between sweet and funky with its fish sauce-kissed caramel glaze. When cooked in a cast-iron skillet, the pork turns charred and caramelized in the best of ways.

Serves 6

PREP TIME:
20 minutes, plus overnight to marinate

COOK TIME:
25 minutes, plus 5 minutes to cool

½ cup plus 2 tablespoons granulated sugar, divided

¼ cup boiling water

2 tablespoons fish sauce

2 shallots, finely chopped

3 garlic cloves, minced

¾ teaspoon kosher salt

½ teaspoon freshly ground black pepper

2½ pounds boneless pork shoulder, trimmed and cut into 1-inch cubes

1 tablespoon vegetable oil

3 cups cooked rice, for serving

1. In a large Dutch oven, heat ½ cup of the sugar over medium-high heat on the stovetop, swirling the pan until the sugar dissolves and turns into molten caramel. Remove from the heat and whisk in the boiling water, stirring gently until the caramel dissolves, 5 to 7 minutes. Let cool, about 5 minutes.

2. Add the cooled caramel to a food processor along with the remaining 2 tablespoons of sugar, fish sauce, shallots, garlic, salt, and pepper. Puree the mixture until smooth.

3. Place the pork cubes in a large, resealable bag. Pour in the puree, seal the bag, squish the contents around to evenly distribute the caramel, and transfer to the refrigerator to marinate overnight.

4. Remove the pork from the refrigerator and drain, reserving the marinade. Pat the pork dry with paper towels.

5. In a 12-inch cast-iron grill pan, heat the oil over high heat until shimmering. Working in three batches, add the pork and about 1½ teaspoons of marinade per batch. Cook, turning once, until the meat is slightly charred and cooked through, about 2 minutes. Serve immediately with the rice.

Milk-Braised Pork Roast

ONE POT

This milk-braised pork is as inviting as the day is long. Serve it with mashed potatoes or steamed bread dumplings. If you quickly boil and butter some green beans, you have the perfect meal for a weekend supper or intimate gathering.

Serves 6

PREP TIME:
10 minutes,
plus 1 hour to
rest

COOK TIME:
2 hours
20 minutes

1 tablespoon finely
   chopped fresh sage
2 fresh thyme sprigs
1 tablespoon finely
   chopped fresh
   rosemary
1 garlic clove, minced
½ teaspoon kosher salt

¼ teaspoon freshly
   ground black pepper
1 (2½-pound) pork loin
2 tablespoons extra-virgin
   olive oil
2 tablespoons unsalted butter
2 to 3 cups whole milk,
   plus more as needed

1. In a small bowl, combine the sage, thyme sprigs, rosemary, garlic, salt, and pepper. Put the pork on a large plate and rub with seasoning mixture. Cover and transfer to the refrigerator to rest for at least 1 hour and up to overnight.

2. In a large Dutch oven, heat the oil and butter until the butter starts to foam. Add the pork and sear until it is golden brown on all sides, about 10 minutes. Reduce the heat to medium-low.

3. Add 2 cups of milk and bring to a low simmer. Baste the meat, cover, and cook, turning the roast occasionally for about 2 hours. Add additional milk ¼ cup at a time, as needed, if the pan liquid begins to look dry. When most of the liquid has evaporated and an instant-read thermometer inserted into the center reads 160°F, transfer the pork to a cutting board and tent with foil.

4. Skim the fat from the sauce and discard the thyme sprigs. Add an additional cup of milk if the liquid is low and continue simmering the sauce uncovered over medium heat, stirring constantly and scraping the browned bits from the bottom of the pan. After about 10 minutes, the sauce should be reduced by ⅔ and the liquid will appear lightly browned and stippled with small, golden-brown curds. Taste and adjust the seasoning, if needed.

5. Carve the pork into ⅓-inch slices and serve with the sauce.

Pork Agrodolce

ONE POT

Marinated and then blanketed in sweet, sour, and salty flavors of the Italian condiment *agrodolce*, this punchy, pan-seared, oven-baked pork can be served alongside pasta or mashed potatoes. *Buon appetito!*

 Serves 4

PREP TIME:
15 minutes,
plus
15 minutes
to rest and
4 hours to
marinate

COOK TIME:
45 minutes,
plus
10 minutes
to rest

2 (1-pound) pork tenderloins
Kosher salt
Freshly ground black pepper
¼ cup capers, drained
1 tablespoon capers brine
½ cup pitted green olives
½ cup pitted prunes, torn in half
¼ cup red wine vinegar
1 cup dry white wine,
   such as pinot grigio
⅓ cup light brown sugar, packed

8 garlic cloves, finely chopped
2 dried bay leaves
2 tablespoons fresh oregano,
   minced, or 1 tablespoon
   dried oregano
¼ cup extra-virgin
   olive oil, divided
½ cup chicken broth
1 tablespoon unsalted butter
¼ cup finely chopped
   fresh flat-leaf parsley

1. Season the pork with salt and pepper and allow it to rest for 15 minutes. In a large, resealable plastic bag, combine the capers, brine, olives, prunes, red wine vinegar, white wine, brown sugar, garlic, bay leaves, oregano, and 3 tablespoons of the oil. Add the pork, seal the bag, and squish the contents around to combine and distribute the marinade. Transfer to the refrigerator to marinate for at least 4 hours and up to overnight.

2. Adjust the rack to the middle position and preheat the oven to 325°F. Remove the pork from the marinade. Reserve the marinade. Pat the meat dry and season with salt and pepper.

3. In a large Dutch oven over medium-high heat, heat the remaining 1 tablespoon of oil until shimmering. Brown the pork, turning occasionally, until golden, 6 to 8 minutes.

4. Remove from the heat, pour the marinade on top, and transfer to the oven to cook. Bake 25 to 30 minutes, basting halfway through. Remove from the oven when an instant-read thermometer inserted into the thickest part registers 145°F. Transfer to a cutting board to rest for 10 minutes.

5. In the Dutch oven over medium heat on the stovetop, add the broth, butter, and parsley to the pan and simmer, scraping up browned bits from the bottom of the pan. Continue cooking until slightly reduced, about 5 minutes. Taste and adjust the seasoning, if needed.

6. Slice the pork and serve, spooning the pan sauce on top.

Sticky Chinese-Inspired Char Sui Pork

MAKE AHEAD

Let this vibrant, flavorful pork marinate overnight to infuse it with sweet, salty flavor. Roasting it on a rack helps the meat cook evenly and prevents burning, as does the water that gets added to the pan.

 Serves 8

PREP TIME:
10 minutes,
plus 8 hours to
marinate

COOK TIME:
50 minutes,
plus
5 minutes
to rest

⅛ cup granulated sugar
⅛ cup dark brown sugar, packed
1¼ teaspoons kosher salt
½ teaspoon white pepper
½ teaspoon five-spice powder
½ teaspoon sesame oil
1 tablespoon soy sauce
1 teaspoon dark soy sauce,
   or additional teaspoon
   standard soy sauce

1 tablespoon hoisin sauce
2 teaspoons molasses
⅛ teaspoon red food coloring
3 garlic cloves, minced
1 (3-pound) pork shoulder, cut
   into large, even chunks
2½ cups water, divided
   and as needed
2 tablespoons honey
3 cups cooked rice, for serving

1. In a large resealable bag, combine the granulated sugar, brown sugar, salt, white pepper, five-spice powder, sesame oil, soy sauce, dark soy sauce, hoisin sauce, molasses, food coloring, and garlic. Seal the bag and squish the contents around to combine. Reserve 2 tablespoons of the marinade in the refrigerator for later use. Add the pork to the bag, seal the bag, and squish the contents around again, taking care to evenly distribute the marinade over the meat. Refrigerate for 8 hours.

2. Adjust the rack to the upper-middle position and preheat the oven to 475°F. Using a large roasting pan outfitted with a metal rack, line the pan with foil.

3. Remove the pork from the marinade. Discard the liquid and pat the meat dry. Pour 1½ cups of the water into the bottom of the pan and transfer the meat to the oven to roast for 25 minutes.

4. In a small bowl, combine the reserved marinade with the honey and 1 tablespoon of the water while the meat is roasting.

Continued ▷→

5. After the meat has cooked for 25 minutes, baste the pork shoulder generously with the reserved marinade mixture. Add another ½ cup of the water if the bottom of the pan looks dry. Rotate the pan 180 degrees and roast for an additional 15 minutes. Flip the meat, baste, and roast for 10 minutes more, or until the meat is nicely caramelized and an instant-read thermometer inserted into the meat reads 160°F. Remove from the oven and allow the meat to rest for 5 minutes before serving with the rice.

TROUBLESHOOTING TIP: Don't have a metal rack? Use 5-inch sheets of foil instead, forming long strips into circles and placing them beneath the pork to elevate it from the bottom of the pan.

Feijoada

MAKE AHEAD · ONE POT

Smoky and hearty, this iconic Brazilian dish is comfort food at its finest. Serve yours with garlic rice, zingy tomato-onion vinaigrette, and *farofa* (toasted cassava flour).

Serves 8

PREP TIME:
25 minutes,
plus overnight
to soak

COOK TIME:
2 hours
40 minutes,
plus 5 minutes
to rest

2 tablespoons vegetable oil

1 large onion, finely chopped

5 large garlic cloves, minced

1½ pounds dried black beans, soaked overnight and drained

4 dried bay leaves

1½ quarts water, plus more as needed, divided

1 pound linguica sausage or dry Spanish chorizo

½ pound boneless pork shoulder

1½ pounds smoked pork chops, bone-in, ⅛-inch thick

1 smoked ham hock

6 dry-cured chorizo links, halved

1½ teaspoons kosher salt

1. In a large Dutch oven, heat the oil over medium heat. Add the onion and sauté, stirring occasionally, for 5 minutes. Add the garlic and cook 1 minute more. Add the beans, bay leaves, and 1½ quarts of water. Reduce the heat to low and simmer, uncovered, for 1 hour.

2. Add the linguica sausage, pork shoulder, pork chops, ham, and chorizo and continue cooking for 1½ hours more, or until the beans are tender. If the liquid gets low, add ¼ cup of water at a time until the beans are sufficiently moist. During the last 30 minutes, add the salt.

3. Discard the bay leaves and transfer the linguica sausage, pork shoulder, pork chops, ham, and chorizo to a cutting board. Cut or shred the meat, discarding any bones and bits of fat. Return the meat to the Dutch oven. Taste and adjust the seasoning, if needed. Allow the meat to rest for 5 minutes. Ladle into bowls and serve.

SUBSTITUTION TIP: Can't find linguica or Spanish chorizo? Garlic sausage or kielbasa work, too.

Dan Dan Noodles

Dan dan noodles are a Sichuan staple, one I'd eat almost any day of the week. For this version, I suggest toasting the noodles lightly. Just heat a swirl of vegetable oil in a hot skillet, add the cooked noodles, and toss them with tongs until they start getting a little crunchy.

Serves 4

PREP TIME:
20 minutes

COOK TIME:
30 minutes

2½ tablespoons vegetable oil, divided
1 pound ground pork
1 medium onion, finely chopped
1 celery stalk, finely chopped
1 large carrot, finely chopped
1 teaspoon toasted sesame oil
1 teaspoon chili oil
2 garlic cloves, minced

2 tablespoons Shaoxing wine (Chinese rice wine), rice wine, or dry sherry
½ teaspoon Chinese five-spice powder
1 tablespoon hoisin sauce
1 teaspoon soy sauce
1 pound Chinese egg noodles, blanched in hot water, drained

1. In a large skillet over medium-high heat, heat ½ tablespoon of the vegetable oil until it is shimmering. Add the pork and brown, breaking into small bits, until cooked through and lightly golden, about 7 minutes.

2. Nudge the meat to the side of the pan and add the onion, celery, and carrot. Cook, stirring occasionally, until tender, about 7 minutes. Reduce the heat to medium and add the sesame oil, chili oil, and garlic. Cook for 1 minute, stirring constantly.

3. Add the Shaoxing wine. Simmer for 2 minutes. Add the five-spice powder, hoisin sauce, and soy sauce. Stir and reduce the heat to low, cooking for 5 minutes more.

4. In another large skillet, add 1 tablespoon of vegetable oil over medium-high heat. When oil is shimmering and easily coats the pan, spread the noodles in the skillet in a thin, even layer. Fry undisturbed for 5 minutes. Flip noodles over, add another tablespoon of oil around the perimeter of the skillet, and let the other side crisp up. To serve, toss the meat and vegetables with the noodles.

INGREDIENT TIP: Springy and slightly chewy Chinese egg noodles are made from wheat flour, water, and egg. Look for thin, fresh ones in the supermarket's produce department or packaged dry ones in the Asian section of most grocery stores. They should contain egg, rather than a food-coloring tint. I'd also suggest adding 1 teaspoon of dark soy sauce and 1½ teaspoons of oyster sauce to the mix, provided you have access to a well-stocked supermarket or international grocer.

4

LAMB
AND VEAL

Although less commonly eaten in the United States, lamb and veal are solid alternatives to beef, pork, and chicken. They can be a bit of a splurge, but they're absolutely delicious. Lamb is grass-fed more often than many other animals raised for meat; the sheep are often left to graze. Most cuts of veal are lower in fat than beef. If these meats are not already in your repertoire, they should be. The recipes in this chapter endeavor to send you down that path.

◀────◀◀◀ PANFRIED LAMB CHOPS WITH SALSA VERDE, PAGE 110

COMMON CUTS
LAMB

Ground Lamb

Usually a combination of shoulder meat and trimmings from other cuts, ground lamb can be grilled, panfried, or boiled until it reaches an internal temperature of 160°F.

Lamb Chops

Loin chops look like small T-bone steaks and offer a generous portion of meat. Pricier and incredibly tender, rib chops are cut from the rack and feature long bones on the side. Meanwhile, budget-friendly shoulder chops are larger, chewier, and fattier. Panfry, roast, broil, or grill chops until they reach 130°F on an instant-read thermometer.

Lamb Shoulder

A less-expensive cut, lamb shoulder is tougher and chewier than the leg. If the lamb is particularly young, however, cooking turns it succulent. A boneless shoulder is easier to carve, though bone-in wins on flavor as always. Lamb shoulder can be slow-roasted whole or cut into chunks for braising.

Leg of Lamb

An ideal centerpiece for a special meal, leg of lamb comes from the hindquarters and typically weighs between 8 and 10 pounds. Although boneless leg of lamb is easier to carve (especially when butterflied), choosing a bone-in cut yields more flavor. Leg of lamb can be stuffed, roasted, and grilled. Cook it until it reaches an internal temperature of 130°F for medium-rare or 145°F for medium-well.

Top Round

This thick cut comes from a large muscle of the leg and can be cut into steaks, cubed for kebabs, panfried, grilled, or roasted whole and served thinly sliced.

VEAL

Ground Veal

Ground veal is commonly found at grocery stores and butcher shops. Tender but lean, it's best combined with fattier ground beef or pork. Use it to make burgers or meat loaf, or try adding it into a Bolognese sauce.

Stew Meat

Cubed veal stew meat is sourced from the front shoulder of the animal. This cost-effective cut contains lots of connective tissue and muscular structure, so braising it breaks it down and results in a lush, gelatinous sauce.

Veal Chops

Bone-in, meaty, and thick, veal chops are available two ways. Rib chops come from the loin; less-expensive porterhouse chops come from the rack. Both cuts are great for broiling, roasting, or grilling. Cook until they reach an internal temperature of 130°F for medium-rare.

Veal Cutlets

Thin, boneless veal cutlets are taken from the leg of the animal. Avoid cutlets from the shoulder, as they're too sinewy to be tender. Treat this cut as you would any other thin, breaded cutlet, seasoning it well and using a three-part dredging process that includes seasoned flour, egg, and bread crumbs.

Veal Shanks

Veal shanks come from the calf's lower leg. Ideal for braising, this bone-in cut should be browned on the stovetop and then finished in a low oven, in braising liquid, for hours. Rendered fork-tender, it can stand up to big, bold flavors.

WHAT COULD
GO WRONG?

Lamb

Q: Does it matter which cut I choose?
Knowing your cuts and choosing the right one for your dish is essential since each one cooks differently. Ask your local butcher when in doubt.

Q: Can I choose a boneless cut over one that's bone-in?
Although boneless meat is easier to carve, you'll sacrifice flavor. Besides, bone-in roasts are a sight to behold. Don't be shy about carving a roast, such as a leg, tableside.

Q: Carving a bone-in leg of lamb seems hard. How do I do it?
Begin with the bone facing toward you. Cut a few slices from the outside edge so you have a flat surface for resting the leg. Rotate the lamb so the bone is perpendicular to your knife. Begin slicing the meat, cutting all the way down to the bone. Don't worry if a lot of meat stays attached to the bone. When you're done slicing, just turn your knife parallel to the bone and cut along the top of the bone to release the slices that remain. Flip the leg over and repeat.

Q: Can I cook lamb right from the refrigerator?
Never cook protein from the refrigerator. Bringing it to room temperature promotes even cooking and juicy results. Remove it from the refrigerator an hour before cooking.

Q: Is there a such thing as marinating lamb too long?
Marinating lamb does infuse the meat with extra flavor. If you marinate your cut too long, however, acidic ingredients render the meat's surface mealy and mushy. Try to marinate for just a few hours, and don't marinate for more than 24 hours. When it comes to thinner cuts, like lamb chops, 15 to 20 minutes of marinating should be enough.

Q: Do I have to trim lamb?

To minimize lamb's gamy flavor, don't forget to trim your cuts: much of that unwelcome edge comes from the fat. This is especially true of cuts like lamb shoulder and leg of lamb.

Q: Is there such a thing as cooking lamb too long?

To keep lamb juicy, avoid making it well-done. It should be removed from the oven when the internal temperature reaches 145°F at most. Like beef steak, most people prefer lamb that's cooked to medium-rare (130°F to 135°F).

Q: Can I carve lamb as soon as it's done cooking?

It is crucial to let meat rest after cooking. When meat cooks, the proteins and fibers inside the meat seize up, release moisture, and become firm. When the meat rests, those fibers relax and reabsorb the moisture they released. If you cut into lamb—or any meat—too soon, the juices spill out onto the cutting board instead.

Q: What do I need to watch for when carving lamb?

If you're carving lamb, it's integral to cut against the grain. Otherwise, you'll end up with chewy meat. Position your knife so as to make perpendicular slices against the grain. This way, the meat will be more tender.

Veal

Q: Can I use ground veal by itself?

Ground veal is tender, but very lean, so it's best combined with another, fattier cut of meat, like 20 percent fat beef or pork.

Q: Do I cook veal the same way as beef?

Veal is tender and comes from young calves. It does not have the fat and marbling of beef; therefore, the cooking requirements differ. Moist, slower cooking for veal is ideal.

Q: How do I know if veal is fresh?

Choose fresh veal in the case that is grayish pink in color and firm to the touch. If the veal has been vacuum-packaged and placed in a self-serve case, a fresh cut is likely to be a deeper red hue because it has not been exposed to as much oxygen. Look for unpunctured packages that are cool to the touch and have little to no excess liquid.

Rosemary-Garlic Grilled Lamb Chops

5 INGREDIENTS OR FEWER · ONE POT

Tender lamb chops—or lamb cutlets—are the most expensive cut of lamb. When left together and cooked whole, rack of lamb makes for an impressive special occasion meal. Here, a simple, lively marinade and a quick, foolproof technique help you make the most of the luxurious cut.

Serves 4

PREP TIME:
5 minutes,
plus 1 hour to
marinate

COOK TIME:
10 minutes,
plus 5 minutes
to rest

2 large garlic cloves, whole
1 tablespoon fresh rosemary
  leaves, whole
1 teaspoon kosher salt
½ teaspoon freshly
  ground black pepper
2 tablespoons extra-virgin
  olive oil

8 (1-inch thick) lamb loin chops
  or frenched lamb rib chops
Nonstick cooking
  spray (optional)
½ lemon, cut into wedges

1. In the bowl of a blender, add the garlic, rosemary, salt, pepper, and oil. Puree until smooth.

2. Place the lamb chops into a large, resealable bag and pour the marinade on top. Seal the bag and squish the contents around to combine. Transfer to the refrigerator to marinate for at least 1 hour and up to 4 hours.

3. Light a charcoal grill or heat a gas grill on medium-high heat (375°F). Alternatively, spray a grill pan with nonstick cooking spray and heat it on the stovetop. Sear the lamb chops for 3 to 4 minutes on the first side, flip them, and continue cooking them for 2 to 3 minutes or until an instant-read thermometer inserted into the center reads 135°F for medium-rare or 145°F for medium.

4. Transfer to a plate. Tent with foil and let rest for 5 minutes. Serve with lemon wedges.

> **SUBSTITUTION TIP:** If you don't have fresh rosemary, use 1 teaspoon of dried rosemary instead.

Grilled Lamb Kofta

FREEZER-FRIENDLY · MAKE AHEAD

These ultra-flavorful, Mediterranean-style kebabs are fantastic tucked into pita bread and served with pickled banana peppers, mint-laced tzatziki, and slivers of red onion. Make a double batch, freeze the meat uncooked, and thaw it the next time you have company.

Serves 4 to 6
___

PREP TIME:
15 minutes, plus 1 hour to chill
___

COOK TIME:
10 minutes

½ pound ground lamb
½ pound ground beef
1 large onion, grated
3 medium garlic cloves, minced
1 large egg, lightly beaten
½ cup minced flat-leaf parsley
1 teaspoon ground cumin
1 teaspoon ground allspice
½ teaspoon ground sumac (optional)
⅛ teaspoon ground cinnamon

1 teaspoon dried mint
1 teaspoon ground hot pepper, such as Aleppo pepper or ancho chili powder
¾ teaspoon kosher salt
½ teaspoon freshly ground black pepper
6 wooden skewers, soaked in water
Nonstick cooking spray

1. In a medium bowl, combine by hand the lamb, beef, onion, garlic, egg, parsley, cumin, allspice, sumac (if using), cinnamon, mint, hot pepper, salt, and pepper. Mix gently but thoroughly and do not over-mix.

2. Fill a small bowl with warm water. Divide the meat mixture into 6 portions. With wet hands to prevent sticking, form the meat into cigar-shaped kebabs about 4 inches long. Thread each kebab onto a skewer, pinching the sides and flattening the meat as you go to help it adhere to the skewer. Chill the meat in the refrigerator, covered, for at least 1 hour.

3. Light a charcoal grill or heat a gas grill on medium-high heat (375°F). Alternatively, spray a grill pan with nonstick cooking spray and heat it on medium-high heat on the stovetop. Once the grill is hot, cook the skewers, flipping periodically until the meat is cooked through, 8 or 9 minutes, or until an instant-read thermometer registers 160°F. Remove the skewers from the grill and serve.

INGREDIENT TIP: Ground sumac is readily available at most international markets and online. If you can't find it, substitute za'atar seasoning or ½ teaspoon fine lemon zest.

Mediterranean Grilled Lamb Shoulder

Lamb shoulder is delicious when grilled over an open fire. Another bonus? It's an affordable cut. Slicing it into more manageable pieces speeds up the cooking time, and marinating it for a few hours infuses the meat with an herbaceous zing of flavor. Serve it with tomatoes, slivers of onion, and tzatziki.

Serves 8

PREP TIME:
15 minutes,
plus 4 hours to
marinate

COOK TIME:
15 minutes,
plus 5 minutes
to rest

1 teaspoon kosher salt,
  plus more to season

1 teaspoon freshly ground black
  pepper, plus more to season

2 medium onions,
  coarsely chopped

2 garlic cloves, chopped

2 tablespoons fresh dill,
  tough stems removed

½ cup fresh mint leaves,
  coarsely chopped

¾ cup fresh oregano leaves,
  coarsely chopped

¾ cup red wine vinegar

¼ cup extra-virgin olive oil

1 (3- to 4-pound) boneless
  lamb shoulder

Nonstick cooking
  spray (optional)

1. In the bowl of a food processor or blender, combine the salt, pepper, onions, garlic, dill, mint, oregano, red wine vinegar, and oil and pulse to form a coarse paste. Reserve.

2. Use a sharp knife to cut the lamb shoulder into 5 or 6 smaller pieces at its natural seams. Place the meat in a large, resealable bag. Add the marinade, seal the bag, and squish the contents around to evenly distribute it over the meat. Transfer to the refrigerator to marinate at least 4 hours and up to overnight.

3. Gently pat the meat dry with paper towels and discard the remaining marinade. Light a charcoal grill or heat a gas grill on medium-high heat (375°F). Alternatively, spray a grill pan with nonstick cooking spray and heat it on medium-high heat on the stovetop. Once the grill is hot, place the meat on the grill, keeping the adhered marinade in place. Cook for 10 to 15 minutes, flipping often and watching for staggered cooking times. Remove from the grill when an instant-read thermometer inserted into the center of each piece reads 135°F for medium-rare or 145°F for medium.

4. Transfer the meat to a cutting board, season with salt and pepper, and let rest for 5 minutes. Cut into thin slices and serve.

Aromatic Lamb-Fry

ONE POT

This fragrant lamb-fry gets on the table fast thanks to a shortcut: time-saving garam masala spice blend. Garnish the dish with cilantro and serve with warm roti or parathas, found in the freezer section of well-stocked international markets.

Serves 4

PREP TIME:
15 minutes

COOK TIME:
25 minutes

2 pounds leg of lamb, cubed

1 teaspoon kosher salt, plus more to season

½ teaspoon freshly ground black pepper, plus more to season

3 tablespoons vegetable oil

2 cups thinly sliced onion

2 garlic cloves, minced

1 teaspoon minced ginger

1 serrano chile, stemmed and minced

2 tablespoons garam masala

½ teaspoon freshly squeezed lemon juice

2 cups cooked basmati or white rice, for serving

1. Season the meat with salt and pepper. In a large nonstick skillet over medium-high heat, heat the oil until shimmering. Cook the onion, stirring often, until nicely browned on the edges, about 5 to 7 minutes.

2. Reduce the heat to medium and add the pepper, garlic, ginger, and chile. Stir for 1 minute before adding the garam masala. Continue cooking until the spices are fragrant, about 1 minute.

3. Add the lamb and salt and cook over medium heat, stirring frequently, until the lamb is cooked through, about 10 to 15 minutes.

4. Stir in the lemon juice, remove from the heat, and serve with the rice.

VARIATION TIP: For a twist, brown 8 slices of bacon in the skillet, cooking them until they are crisp on both sides. Remove the slices and drain them on a paper-towel-lined plate. Cut back the oil in the recipe to 1 tablespoon, using the bacon fat in its place. Crumble and add the reserved bacon during the last 5 minutes of cooking.

Panfried Lamb Chops with Salsa Verde

Although these chops are panfried, they're also great on the grill or cooked in a grill pan. The bright, herby salsa verde that's served alongside will convince even non-lamb-lovers to indulge—and perhaps even request the recipe.

Serves 4

PREP TIME:
15 minutes,
plus
30 minutes
to rest

COOK TIME:
10 minutes,
plus 5 minutes
to rest

FOR THE LAMB

8 (1-inch-thick) lamb loin chops
   or frenched lamb rib chops
2 tablespoons extra-virgin
   olive oil

Kosher salt
Freshly ground black pepper

FOR THE SALSA VERDE

1 small shallot, finely chopped
2 cups loosely packed fresh
   mint leaves, finely chopped
½ cup fresh finely chopped
   fresh flat-leaf parsley leaves
2 tablespoons fresh tarragon
   leaves, finely chopped
¼ cup crushed red
   pepper flakes
2 teaspoons grated lemon zest

1 tablespoon capers, drained
   and finely chopped, plus
   1 teaspoon caper brine
2 medium garlic cloves,
   finely minced
½ teaspoon kosher salt
½ teaspoon freshly
   ground black pepper
½ cup extra-virgin olive oil
   plus 1 tablespoon, divided

TO MAKE THE LAMB

1. On a 9-by-13-inch baking sheet, rub the lamb with the olive oil and season with salt and pepper. Let the lamb rest on the counter for 30 minutes.

TO MAKE THE SALSA VERDE

2. In a small bowl, combine the shallot, mint, parsley, tarragon, red pepper flakes, lemon zest, capers, garlic, salt, and pepper. Slowly whisk in ½ cup of the oil. Reserve.

3. In a large skillet, heat the remaining 1 tablespoon of the oil over medium-high heat. When shimmering, sear the loin chops for 6 to 8 minutes for medium-rare, flipping halfway through. If using rib chops, cook for 3 to 4 minutes for medium-rare, flipping halfway through.

4. Transfer the meat to a platter. Tent with foil and allow it to rest for 5 minutes. Serve with the salsa verde.

INGREDIENT TIP: Select chops with light red, finely textured meat and smooth, evenly distributed white fat.

Slow-Cooked Lamb Barbacoa

FREEZER-FRIENDLY · MAKE AHEAD · ONE POT

Cooked in a single pot on the stovetop and then in the oven, this one-pot meal is the gift that keeps on giving. It can be prepared and reheated or frozen in an airtight container for up to 3 months.

Serves 6

PREP TIME:
30 minutes

COOK TIME:
3 hours
25 minutes

8 tomatillos, husked and cored

1 serrano chile, stemmed

8 garlic cloves, unpeeled

1 medium onion, halved, with ½ finely chopped, for serving, divided

2 tablespoons ground ancho chili powder

2 tablespoons ground guajillo chili powder

½ teaspoon ground cumin

¼ teaspoon ground cinnamon

¾ teaspoon kosher salt, plus more to season

1 teaspoon ground black pepper, plus more to season

1 teaspoon dried Mexican oregano

1 teaspoon dried thyme

3 tablespoons apple cider vinegar

1 tablespoon light brown sugar, packed

1½ cups low-sodium chicken broth

1 (15-ounce) can diced tomatoes with their juices

1 tablespoon vegetable oil

3 pounds boneless leg of lamb, cut into chunks

20 corn tortillas, warmed, for serving

½ cup roughly chopped cilantro, for serving

Lime wedges, for serving

1. In a large Dutch oven over medium-high heat on the stovetop, cook the tomatillos, serrano chile, garlic, and the unchopped half of the onion, turning often until the ingredients are charred on all sides, 12 to 15 minutes.

2. Peel the charred garlic. Transfer all the charred vegetables to a blender. Add the ancho powder, guajillo chili powder, cumin, cinnamon, salt, pepper, oregano, thyme, apple cider vinegar, brown sugar, broth, and diced tomatoes. Puree until smooth and reserve.

3. Adjust the oven rack to the lower-middle position and preheat the oven to 300°F. Add the oil to the Dutch oven and heat over medium-high heat on the stovetop. Season the lamb with salt and pepper. When the oil is shimmering, brown the meat on all sides, working in batches, about 8 minutes.

4. Pour the reserved charred vegetable sauce over the meat. Bring to a boil. Then, cover and transfer to the oven to braise for 3 hours, or until the meat is fork-tender. Remove from the oven and shred meat.

5. Serve with tortillas, cilantro, lime wedges, and remaining ½ of the finely chopped onion.

Wiener Schnitzel

An alternative version of this beloved, panfried Viennese-inspired dish can be prepared with pork (Panfried Pork Schnitzel, page 88), while thicker fried pork (Pork Tonkatsu, page 66) is a staple in Japan. Indeed, some form of breaded, panfried meat is popular virtually everywhere in the world. Enjoy the Austrian take!

Serves 4
——

PREP TIME:
15 minutes,
plus
15 minutes
to chill
——

COOK TIME:
10 minutes

4 (5-ounce) veal cutlets
¼ cup all-purpose flour
½ teaspoon all-purpose seasoning, such as Lawry's
1 teaspoon garlic salt
1 teaspoon freshly ground black pepper, divided
2 large eggs

4 cups plain bread crumbs
1 teaspoon paprika
1 teaspoon kosher salt
1 tablespoon unsalted butter
2 tablespoons vegetable oil
½ lemon, cut into wedges

1. Working one cutlet at a time, place the cutlets between two sheets of plastic wrap and, using a meat mallet or rolling pin, pound them to a ¼-inch thickness.

2. Gather three small, shallow bowls. In the first, combine the flour, all-purpose seasoning, garlic salt, and ½ teaspoon of the pepper. In the second, whisk the eggs with a fork. In the third, combine the bread crumbs, paprika, salt, and remaining ½ teaspoon of the pepper.

3. Lightly dredge each cutlet in the flour, then dip in the egg. Then dredge in the bread crumbs, pressing the bread crumbs onto the meat to coat evenly. Set the cutlets on a baking sheet and transfer them to the refrigerator for 15 minutes to help the breading adhere.

4. In a large skillet over medium-high heat, heat the butter and oil until hot. Add the cutlets to the pan and cook until golden, about 3 minutes per side. Transfer the meat to paper towels to drain and lightly season with salt. Serve with lemon wedges.

PREP TIP: This dish is best enjoyed fresh and crispy, so resist the temptation to make it in advance.

Veal Parmesan

ONE POT

This weekight-ready dish is the kind of meal the whole family will love. Make the bright one-pot dish even livelier by sprinkling torn basil leaves on top. And, of course, serve it with extra Parmesan cheese.

Serves 4

PREP TIME:
15 minutes

COOK TIME:
25 minutes

4 (5-ounce) veal cutlets
½ teaspoon kosher salt,
  plus more to season
¼ teaspoon freshly
  ground black pepper,
  plus more to season
1 egg
½ cup dry, unseasoned
  bread crumbs

½ teaspoon Italian seasoning
⅓ cup grated Parmesan cheese,
  plus 3 tablespoons, divided
1 tablespoon extra-virgin
  olive oil
1 cup homemade or
  store-bought marinara sauce
4 slices whole-milk
  mozzarella cheese

1. Working one cutlet at a time, place the veal between two sheets of plastic wrap and, using a meat mallet or rolling pin, pound to a ½-inch thickness. Season the veal with salt and pepper.

2. Gather two small, shallow bowls. In the first, whisk the egg and season with salt and pepper. In the second, combine the bread crumbs, Italian seasoning, and ⅓ cup of the Parmesan. Season with salt and pepper. Dip each cutlet in the egg, then dredge in the bread crumbs.

3. Adjust the oven rack to the lower-middle position and preheat the oven to 350°F.

4. In a large Dutch oven over medium-high heat on the stovetop, heat the oil until shimmering. Sear each cutlet until golden brown, 2 to 3 minutes per side. Briefly remove the meat from the Dutch oven. Add the marinara sauce. Return the veal to the pan, nestling it into the sauce.

5. Top each cutlet with one slice of mozzarella cheese and the remaining 3 tablespoons of Parmesan cheese. Cover and transfer to the oven to finish cooking, 10 to 15 minutes. If you wish, briefly broil uncovered until bubbly and browned.

Veal Scallopini with Mushrooms

ONE POT

Quick and easy enough for a Tuesday night, this classic, hassle-free Italian dish is also more than worthy of a dinner party. Serve it with oven-roasted potatoes, buttered green beans, and a medium-bodied Italian merlot.

Serves 4

PREP TIME:
10 minutes

COOK TIME:
25 minutes

8 (3-ounce) veal cutlets
¾ teaspoon kosher salt, divided, plus more to season
¾ teaspoon freshly ground black pepper, divided, plus more to season
1 cup all-purpose flour
1 tablespoon extra-virgin olive oil

1 cup sliced baby portabella or white button mushrooms
½ stick unsalted butter, cut into pieces
½ cup dry white wine
1 tablespoon red wine vinegar
1½ lemons, juiced
¼ cup finely chopped fresh flat-leaf parsley leaves

1. Working one cutlet at a time, place the veal between two sheets of plastic wrap and, using a meat mallet or rolling pin, pound to a ½-inch thickness. Season with salt and pepper.

2. In a small, shallow bowl, combine the flour and ½ teaspoon each of salt and pepper. Dredge the meat in the flour mixture.

3. In a large, heavy skillet over medium-high heat, heat the oil until shimmering. Working in two batches, sear the veal until golden brown, 2 to 3 minutes per side. Transfer the meat to a platter and tent with foil to keep warm.

4. Using residual oil, brown the mushrooms, stirring occasionally until soft and lightly browned, about 7 minutes. Move to the side of the skillet and add the butter, cooking until browned and fragrant, about 2 minutes. Add the white wine and bring to a simmer. Cook for 2 minutes, stirring to dislodge browned bits from the bottom of the skillet. Add the red wine vinegar, lemon juice, and ¼ teaspoon each of salt and pepper.

5. Return the veal to the pan and heat through. Serve, spooning the sauce on top and garnish with parsley.

> **SUBSTITUTION TIP:** Veal is relatively expensive and the available cuts at the supermarket are somewhat limited. Feel free to substitute chicken or pork cutlets.

Classic Veal Piccata

ONE POT

Bracing and lively, this classic Italian dish demands a starch of some sort. Try serving it with garlicky angel-hair pasta that's sprinkled with fresh herbs, along with crusty garlic bread and a bottle of chilled pinot gris.

Serves 4

PREP TIME:
15 minutes

COOK TIME:
40 minutes

8 (3-ounce) veal cutlets
½ teaspoon kosher salt, plus more to season
½ teaspoon freshly ground black pepper, plus more to season
1 cup all-purpose flour
1 tablespoon extra-virgin olive oil
3 garlic cloves, minced

½ cup dry white wine, such as pinot grigio
¼ cup capers, drained
½ cup low-sodium chicken broth
4 tablespoons unsalted butter
Juice of 1½ lemons
¼ cup fresh finely chopped fresh flat-leaf parsley leaves

1. Working 1 cutlet at a time, put the veal between two sheets of plastic wrap and, using a meat mallet or rolling pin, pound to a ½-inch thickness. Season the veal with salt and pepper.

2. In a small, shallow bowl, combine the flour, salt, and pepper. Dredge the meat in the flour mixture.

3. In a large nonstick skillet over medium-high heat, heat the oil until shimmering. Working in two batches, sear the veal until golden brown, 2 to 3 minutes per side. Move the meat to a platter and tent with foil to keep warm.

4. Add the garlic to the skillet and sauté for 2 minutes, stirring constantly so it doesn't burn. Add the white wine and capers to the pan and bring to a boil. Allow to simmer for about 5 minutes, and scrape the bottom of the skillet to dislodge the browned bits. When reduced by half, add the broth. Simmer for 5 minutes more. When the mixture is slightly reduced and thickened, add the butter, swirling it into the sauce to combine. Once the butter is melted and bubbly, stir in the lemon juice. Season with salt and pepper to taste. Add the parsley.

5. Serve, spooning the sauce on top.

Veal Marsala

ONE POT

An Italian American classic, veal marsala pairs wonderfully with mashed potatoes or polenta to showcase its layered, balanced sauce. Want to make the dish your own? Try adding 1 ½ teaspoons finely chopped fresh rosemary or use an assortment of mushrooms, such as maitake, hen of the woods, and chanterelles, to the sauce.

Serves 4

PREP TIME:
15 minutes

COOK TIME:
35 minutes

8 (3-ounce) veal cutlets
½ teaspoon kosher salt, plus more to season
½ teaspoon freshly ground black pepper, plus more to season
3 tablespoons unsalted butter, divided
2½ tablespoons extra-virgin olive oil, divided
2 tablespoons finely chopped white onion
4 medium garlic cloves, minced
½ cup baby portabella or white button mushrooms, sliced
⅔ cup sweet marsala
¾ cup low-sodium chicken broth

1. Working one at a time, put each cutlet between two sheets of plastic wrap and, using a meat mallet or rolling pin, pound each to a ½-inch thickness. Season the meat with salt and pepper.

2. In a large nonstick skillet over medium-high heat, heat 1 tablespoon each of the butter and oil. When the butter starts to foam, sear four cutlets at a time until they are golden brown, about 2 minutes per side. In between batches, add an additional ½ tablespoon butter and 1 tablespoon of the oil. Remove the meat to a platter and tent with foil to keep warm.

3. Reduce the heat to medium and add the remaining ½ tablespoon of the olive oil if the bottom of the skillet is dry. Add the onion and stir, dislodging the browned bits from the bottom of the pan. Add the mushrooms and continue cooking until they are soft, about 3 minutes. Add the garlic and sauté for 1 minute more, stirring to prevent burning.

4. Once the liquid has evaporated from the skillet, add the marsala and bring to a boil. When reduced by half, after about 2 minutes, add the broth. Season the liquid with ½ teaspoon each salt and pepper.

5. Return the veal and its juices to the skillet to heat through. Stir in the remaining 1½ tablespoon of the butter. Taste and adjust seasonings. Serve the veal with the sauce spooned on top.

SUBSTITUTION TIP: Although this recipe calls for veal, you can just as easily swap it for chicken or pork.

Slow-Cooked Osso Buco

This storied braise is among the most beloved Northern Italian dishes. Consider serving it with a bright, fresh gremolata (green sauce) on top: Just combine ½ cup chopped fresh flat-leaf parsley, 1 tablespoon grated lemon zest, and 2 cloves minced garlic. The gremolata will cut through the richness.

Serves 4

PREP TIME:
30 minutes

COOK TIME:
3 hours, plus
5 minutes to
rest

4 (12-ounce) veal shanks
1 teaspoon kosher salt,
  plus more to season
½ teaspoon freshly
  ground black pepper,
  plus more to season
1 cup all-purpose flour
  plus 2 tablespoons
1½ tablespoons
  extra-virgin olive oil
1 medium onion, diced
2 carrots, diced
1 celery stalk, diced

1 (28-ounce) can plum
  tomatoes, drained
  and crushed
4 medium garlic cloves,
  finely chopped
1 cup dry red wine, such as
  cabernet sauvignon
4 cups low-sodium
  chicken broth
½ teaspoon dried oregano
4 fresh thyme sprigs
2 dried bay leaves

1. Adjust the oven rack to the lower-middle position and preheat to 350°F. Pat the veal shanks dry using a paper towel. Using kitchen twine, tie the meat once around the center. Season with salt and pepper.

2. In a large, shallow bowl, pour in the flour and season with salt and pepper. Dredge the meat in the flour mixture, shaking off any excess.

3. In a large Dutch oven over medium-high heat on the stovetop, heat the oil until it is lightly smoking. Add the meat and cook without moving until it is well browned on one side, about 5 minutes. Flip and cook until the meat is browned on all sides, about 8 minutes more.

4. Add the onion, carrots, and celery to the Dutch oven. Reduce the heat to medium and cook, stirring occasionally, until the vegetables begin to soften, about 6 minutes. Add the tomatoes and garlic. Stir and continue cooking until fragrant, about 1 minute longer.

5. Add the red wine and simmer until the mixture is reduced by half, about 3 minutes. Add the broth, oregano, thyme sprigs, bay leaves, salt, and pepper. Stir to combine and return to a boil.

6. Cover and transfer to the oven until the meat is fork-tender, about 2½ hours. Remove from the oven, discarding the thyme sprigs, bay leaves, and kitchen twine. Taste and adjust the seasonings, if needed. Let rest for 5 minutes and serve.

5

POULTRY

The go-to protein in most households, poultry takes on the flavor of marinades, crisps up in the oven or on the grill when cooked skin-on, and can be used as leftovers in endless ways. It has a somewhat understated flavor, but that makes it a wonderful canvas for a range of tastes and cooking techniques. From impressive whole birds to Fourth of July–ready fare, you'll never get stuck in a rut, provided you use your imagination and favorite ingredients as a guide.

← PANFRIED NASHVILLE HOT CHICKEN THIGHS, PAGE 140

COMMON CUTS

Chicken or Turkey Breast or Fillet

Chicken breast is sold by the half (split) breast or full breast, either bone-in or deboned. Turkey breast typically includes the whole bone-in break with ribs, a portion of the wing meat, and part of the back and neck skin. It can be panfried, stuffed, baked, coated, or wrapped, making it an incredibly versatile choice. Smaller bits can also be added to soups and stews, stir-fries, and potpies. Be careful not to overcook or the meat will be dry.

Chicken or Turkey Drumstick

Affordable and easy to cook, drumsticks are produced by cutting the whole leg between the tibia and the femur and removing the thigh. Ideal for barbecuing, roasting, or frying, drumsticks can be battered or rolled in bread crumbs, too.

Chicken or Turkey Leg

Obtained by cutting at the natural seam through the hip, a chicken leg includes the thigh and drumstick. Suited to grilling, they can also be used to make homemade soup and broth.

Chicken or Turkey Thigh

A thigh is produced by cutting a whole leg between the tibia and the femur and removing the drumstick and patella. Perfect for casseroles, grilling, and other slow-cooking methods, it's arguably the tastiest part of a bird. Thighs can be bought bone-in or boneless, with or without skin. Always check that they have reached an internal temperature of 165°F.

Chicken or Turkey Wing

The wing has three parts: the drumette, the wingette or flat, and the tip. A bit meatier, the drumette is the part that was directly attached to the rest of the bird. The wingette or flat is the middle section of the wing. The skin-and-cartilage-heavy tip is, clearly, the tip of the wing. Chicken wing meat is typically sold as an equal mix of wingettes and drumettes, while turkey wings are usually served whole. Both can be fried, roasted, smoked, or barbecued, with or without a marinade or glaze.

Tenders

Also called chicken fingers, chicken strips, or chicken fillets, these strips of white meat are found on either side of the breastbone, under the breast meat. They're a crowd-pleaser, particularly when breaded and fried.

Whole Chicken or Turkey

A whole bird consists of the breast, thighs, drumsticks, wings, back, and abdominal fat. It may or may not include giblets and the neck in its cavity. These parts can be removed and used to make gravy, or simply removed and discarded. Whether you roast the bird whole or break it down into the different cuts yourself, poaching the bird capitalizes on its flavors, while roasting it yields crisp, glistening skin and moist meat. As with all poultry, it should be cooked to an internal temperature of 165F.

WHAT COULD GO WRONG?

Q: Is it okay to buy previously frozen meat?
If you want to enjoy juicy chicken, it's essential to lock in its water content. When chicken is previously frozen, the meat can dry out. Look for the "fresh, never frozen" label on packaged chicken.

Q: Is it okay to remove turkey skin before cooking?
For the juiciest results possible, leave the skin on. It will crisp up and help the meat retain more fat and more moisture.

Q: Can I cook chicken when it's cold?
As is the case with other proteins, never cook chicken directly from the refrigerator. Doing so can lead to uneven, overcooked meat. Take it out of the refrigerator 20 to 30 minutes before cooking to bring down its temperature.

Q: When cooking poultry, why does having a hot pan matter?
A superhot pan is essential to get a nice sear and achieve caramelization. Just remember to place the piece of poultry breast-side down. To ensure the meat ends up extra-juicy, halfway through cooking you can add additional fat, such as a pat of butter or an oil with a high smoking point like canola or grapeseed oil.

Classic Roast Chicken

5 INGREDIENTS OR FEWER · ONE POT

Roast chicken is one of life's simplest and most comforting culinary pleasures. Start checking your chicken after about 40 minutes to make sure it's not too dark. Very loosely tent it with foil if it's browning too quickly. Then remove the foil and let the skin crisp up again during the last 10 minutes of cooking.

Serves 4

PREP TIME:
5 minutes

COOK TIME:
1 hour
30 minutes,
plus
10 minutes
to rest

1 (3- to 3½-pound)
  whole chicken
Kosher salt
Freshly ground black pepper

1½ tablespoons
  extra-virgin olive oil
2½ teaspoons balsamic vinegar

1. Adjust the oven rack to the lower-middle position and preheat the oven to 375°F.

2. Place the chicken on a rack in a roasting pan and season the meat generously with salt and pepper. Drizzle with the olive oil and balsamic vinegar, rubbing it all over to distribute evenly.

3. Transfer the chicken to the oven to cook, basting with the pan juices every 30 minutes. Bake until an instant-read thermometer inserted into the thickest part of thigh registers 175°F and the breast registers at least 165°F, 1 hour, 15 minutes, to 1½ hours.

4. Remove the chicken from the oven, tent it lightly with foil, and allow it to rest for 10 minutes. Meanwhile, skim the fat from the pan juices. Carve the chicken, drizzle it with the pan drippings, and serve.

PREP TIP: If you don't have a rack, take a large sheet of foil and form it into a "donut" shape that's slightly smaller than the chicken itself. Then, place the chicken on top to keep it elevated from the bottom of the pan.

Loi's Chicken Adobo

FREEZER-FRIENDLY · MAKE AHEAD · ONE POT

This homey Filipino mainstay holds a special place in my household. My partner's mom, Loi, prepared it often in their home. I was privileged to watch her make it firsthand. Now, I'm sharing her version—one of countless household variations—with you.

Serves 6

PREP TIME:
10 minutes

COOK TIME:
40 minutes

2 pounds bone-in chicken thighs

1 pound bone-in pork shoulder or country-style ribs

½ cup soy sauce, plus more as needed

½ cup distilled white vinegar, plus more as needed

1 cup water

2 large garlic cloves, crushed

2 dried bay leaves

3 cups cooked white rice, for serving

1. In a large Dutch oven over medium-high heat on the stovetop, combine the chicken, pork, soy sauce, white vinegar, water, garlic, and bay leaves. Bring to a boil, then stir. Reduce heat to medium-low. Cover and simmer, stirring periodically, until meat is tender enough to be pulled from the bone and broth is slightly thickened and gelatinous, about 30 minutes.

2. Remove and discard the bay leaves. Taste and add additional soy and vinegar, if needed.

3. Transfer the meat to a cutting board and pull it from the bones in hunks, discarding the bones and fatty bits. Return the meat to the pan to warm through. Spoon the adobo atop the rice to serve.

PREP TIP: Make a big batch of this and freeze in an airtight container for up to 3 months. It thaws and rewarms beautifully.

Spanish Roast Chicken with Pan Gravy

ONE POT

I made a variation of this chicken for my first real date with Mike, the man who'd become my forever partner and best friend. Here's what I know: The wooing worked. Two weeks later, he flew back from LA to see me again. A cross-country move, a new home, and a son named Anders later, I still credit the chicken.

Serves 4

PREP TIME:
15 minutes

COOK TIME:
1 hour
40 minutes,
plus
10 minutes
to rest

1 (3- to 3½-pound)
  whole chicken
½ teaspoon kosher salt
¼ teaspoon freshly
  ground black pepper
2 teaspoons hot
  smoked paprika
1 teaspoon onion powder
2 tablespoons extra-virgin
  olive oil
¼ cup freshly squeezed
  orange juice
2 teaspoons cornstarch
½ cup water

1. Adjust the oven rack to the lower-middle position and preheat the oven to 375°F. Put the chicken on a rack in a roasting pan.

2. In a small bowl, combine the salt, pepper, paprika, onion powder, olive oil, and orange juice. Using a brush, generously apply the mixture to the bird. If any extra remains, drizzle it on top.

3. Transfer the chicken to the oven to cook, basting with pan juices every 30 minutes, until a thermometer inserted into thickest part of thigh registers 175°F and the breast registers at least 165°F, 1 hour, 15 minutes, to 1½ hours.

4. Remove the chicken from the oven, tent it lightly with foil, and allow it to rest for 10 minutes.

5. While the chicken rests, place the pan on the stove over medium heat and skim the fat from the pan. Bring the juices to a boil. Mix the cornstarch with the water and slowly pour the mixture in, whisking it to avoid lumps. When thickened to a gravy-like consistency, remove sauce from the heat and cover to keep it warm. Carve the chicken and serve it with the gravy.

Oven-Roasted Greek Chicken

MAKE AHEAD

This simple, lemony chicken is cooked on top of potatoes, infusing them with fat and juices from the meat. It's a perfect weeknight dinner that feels homey, hearty, and special.

PREP TIME:
20 minutes

COOK TIME:
1 hour
30 minutes,
plus
10 minutes
to rest

½ cup freshly squeezed
  lemon juice

2 teaspoons grated lemon zest

4 tablespoons extra-virgin
  olive oil

4 large garlic cloves, minced

1 tablespoon chopped
  fresh oregano leaves

1 teaspoon all-purpose
  Greek seasoning (see
  the Substitution Tip)

½ teaspoon fresh thyme
  leaves, stemmed

¾ teaspoon kosher salt,
  plus more to season

1¼ teaspoon freshly
  ground black pepper,
  plus more to season

4 medium russet potatoes, cut
  into 8 wedges lengthwise

1 (3- to 4-pound) chicken,
  cut into 8 pieces

1. Adjust the oven rack to the lower-middle position and preheat the oven to 375°F.

2. In a medium bowl, whisk the lemon juice, lemon zest, olive oil, garlic, oregano, Greek seasoning, thyme, salt, and pepper. Taste and adjust the seasoning of the vinaigrette, if needed.

3. In a large bowl, toss the potatoes with half of the vinaigrette, reserving the rest. Transfer the potatoes to a 9-by-13-inch baking sheet and place in the oven to roast for 20 minutes.

4. Raise the oven temperature to 425°F. Season the chicken with salt and pepper and add to the pan, topping with the remaining vinaigrette. Return the pan to the oven and continue cooking, basting periodically after the first 30 minutes, until an instant-read thermometer inserted into the thickest part registers 165°F, 55 minutes to 1 hour, 5 minutes. Tent the pan loosely with foil if the chicken starts to get too dark.

5. Remove the pan from the oven and let the meat rest for 10 minutes. Serve, spooning the pan sauce on top.

> **SUBSTITUTION TIP:** If you can't find Greek seasoning, replace with ¼ teaspoon each of salt, pepper, onion powder, and granulated garlic.

Pickle-Brined, Panfried Chicken

MAKE AHEAD

Make your fried chicken into a sandwich, topping it with crunchy coleslaw and passing around hot sauce at the table. This is a solid choice for picnics, too, but be sure to let the chicken cool before packing it up so it doesn't lose its crunch.

Serves 4 to 6

———

PREP TIME:
15 minutes, plus 9 hours to brine and marinate

———

COOK TIME:
10 minutes, plus 5 minutes to rest

4 (6-ounce) boneless, skinless chicken breasts

3 cups dill pickle juice

3 cups buttermilk

2 cups all-purpose flour

2 tablespoons cornstarch

1¼ teaspoons kosher salt, plus more to season

1 tablespoon freshly ground black pepper

2 teaspoons garlic powder

¼ teaspoon ground cayenne red pepper

6 cups vegetable oil

1. In a large resealable bag, fully submerge the chicken in the pickle juice. Seal the bag and transfer it to the refrigerator for 8 hours or overnight.

2. Drain and discard the brine. Pour the buttermilk into the bag, submerging the chicken again. Return it to the refrigerator to marinate for at least an hour and up to 8 hours.

3. In a medium bowl, combine the flour, cornstarch, salt, pepper, garlic powder, and cayenne pepper.

4. Remove the chicken from the refrigerator. Drain and discard the buttermilk and pat the chicken dry with paper towels. Dredge the meat in the flour mixture, shaking off any excess. Dredge again.

5. In a large Dutch oven over high heat on the stovetop, heat the oil until it reaches a temperature of 350°F. Fry the chicken until it's golden brown, 6 to 8 minutes, or when an instant-read thermometer inserted into the center of each piece reads 165°F. Remove the chicken from the oil and place on paper towels to rest for at least 5 minutes. Sprinkle with salt and serve.

PREP TIP: If cooking the chicken in larger batches, let the chicken drain briefly on the paper towels. Then, place the chicken on a baking sheet and transfer it to a 200°F oven.

Baked, Stuffed Jalapeño Popper Chicken

MAKE AHEAD

If you like the flavor of jalapeño poppers but don't want the work of individually stuffing them, this recipe is for you. Prepared in a flash and easily doubled or tripled for a group, the chicken can be assembled up to a day in advance. Just pop the prepared meat in a hot oven 30 minutes before you want your meal on the table.

Serves 4

PREP TIME:
15 minutes

COOK TIME:
30 minutes,
plus 5 minutes
to rest

Nonstick cooking spray
1 (8-ounce) package
   cream cheese
½ cup sour cream
1 garlic clove, minced
1 (4-ounce) can
   jalapeños, chopped
½ cup finely shredded
   Parmesan cheese

½ teaspoon kosher salt,
   plus more to season
¼ teaspoon freshly
   ground black pepper,
   plus more to season
4 boneless, skinless
   chicken breasts
½ cup pepper jack cheese

1. Adjust the oven rack to the lower-middle position and preheat the oven to 400°F. Spray an 8-by-8-inch baking dish with nonstick cooking spray.

2. In a small bowl, combine the cream cheese, sour cream, garlic, jalapeños, Parmesan, salt, and pepper.

3. Using a sharp knife, slice along the length of the middle of each breast until it's nearly, but not completely, cut through, opening each breast like a book. Season both sides of the meat with salt and pepper.

4. Working one at a time, put each breast between two sheets of plastic wrap and, using a meat mallet or rolling pin, pound the breasts to a ¼-inch thickness.

5. Spread 2 tablespoons of the sour cream filling over each chicken breast, leaving a ¼-inch border around the edges. Roll each breast lengthwise and secure at ¾-inch intervals with kitchen twine. Season the chicken all over with salt and pepper.

6. Put the chicken in the prepared baking dish. Transfer to the oven to bake for 20 minutes. Top evenly with the pepper jack cheese and bake for an additional 5 to 10 minutes, or when an instant-read thermometer inserted into the center of each piece reads 165°F. Remove from the oven and allow the chicken to rest for 5 minutes. Serve.

SUBSTITUTION TIP: If pepper jack is too spicy for you, use Chihuahua or Monterey Jack cheese instead.

Pan-Seared Lemon Chicken

30 MINUTES OR LESS · ONE POT

This vibrant, citrusy dish is a burst of sunshine on your plate. If you can get your hands on Meyer lemons, by all means use them here. Serve the chicken with a side of rice or oven-roasted potatoes.

Serves 4

——

PREP TIME:
15 minutes

——

COOK TIME:
15 minutes

4 (5-ounce) chicken breasts
Kosher salt
Freshly ground black pepper
⅓ cup all-purpose flour
1 tablespoon extra-virgin
  olive oil
3 tablespoons unsalted
  butter, divided
2 medium garlic cloves, minced
¼ cup dry white wine,
  such as pinot grigio

¼ cup low-sodium
  chicken broth
3 tablespoons freshly
  squeezed lemon juice
½ teaspoon grated lemon zest
1 tablespoon minced
  fresh flat-leaf parsley
½ tablespoon fresh thyme
  leaves, stemmed

1. Working one breast at a time, put the chicken between two pieces of plastic wrap and, using a meat mallet or rolling pin, pound to a ⅓-inch thickness. Season with salt and pepper.

2. In a medium, shallow bowl pour in the flour and season with salt and pepper. Dredge the chicken in the flour mixture, shaking off any excess.

3. In a large skillet over medium-high heat, add the oil and 1 tablespoon of the butter. When the butter starts to foam, add the chicken breasts in a single layer. Cook until golden brown, 4 to 5 minutes per side, or until an instant-read thermometer inserted into the thickest part reads 165°F. Transfer to a platter and tent with foil to keep warm.

4. Reduce the heat to medium and add 1 tablespoon of butter. When melted, add the garlic and sauté, stirring to scrape up the browned bits from the bottom of the skillet. When lightly golden after about 2 minutes, add the white wine. Continue cooking for 2 minutes before adding the broth, lemon juice, and lemon zest. Simmer until the liquids are reduced by half, about 2 minutes more. Add the remaining 1 tablespoon of butter, swirling it into the sauce. Add the parsley and thyme and season with salt and pepper to taste. Serve the chicken with the sauce spooned on top.

SUBSTITUTION TIP: If you don't have wine, you can add an extra ¼ cup of chicken broth in its place.

Baked Chicken Cordon Bleu

FREEZER-FRIENDLY · MAKE AHEAD · ONE POT

Stuffed meat feels fancy. Fortunately, though, the prep work here is not fussy. In fact, this cheesy, smoky, crisp-crusted chicken can be prepared effortlessly any day of the week. Serve it with mashed potatoes or rice and a salad.

Serves 4

PREP TIME:
15 minutes

COOK TIME:
35 minutes,
plus 5 minutes
to rest

Nonstick cooking spray
4 (5-ounce) chicken breasts
½ teaspoon kosher salt,
   plus more to season
½ teaspoon freshly
   ground black pepper,
   plus more to season
1 cup shredded Gruyère or
   Swiss cheese, divided

8 slices deli ham
2 tablespoons Dijon
   mustard, divided
1 cup all-purpose flour
2 large eggs
2 cups coarse, dry panko
   bread crumbs
4 tablespoons unsalted
   butter, melted

1. Preheat the oven to 375°F. Spray an 8-by-8-inch baking dish with nonstick cooking spray.

2. Working one breast at a time, put the chicken between two pieces of plastic wrap and, using a meat mallet or rolling pin, pound to a ¼-inch thickness. Season with salt and pepper.

3. Top each breast evenly with the cheese (¼ cup each), followed by the ham (2 slices each). Slather the ham with the mustard (½ tablespoon on each). Roll up the chicken tightly, tucking in the end and securing the meat with toothpicks.

4. Gather three medium, shallow bowls. In the first, combine the flour, salt, and pepper. In the second, whisk the eggs with a fork. In the third, mix the bread crumbs with the butter, stirring until fully combined.

5. Lightly dredge each breast in the flour, then dip in the egg. Then dredge in the bread crumbs, pressing the bread crumbs onto the chicken to coat evenly.

6. Place the breasts in the prepared baking dish and transfer to the oven to bake for about 30 to 35 minutes, until they are golden brown and an instant-read thermometer registers 165°F when inserted into the center of the rolls.

7. Remove the pan from the oven and allow the meat to rest 5 minutes before serving.

Larb Gai Lettuce Wraps

30 MINUTES OR LESS · MAKE AHEAD

Fresh, healthy, and just plain tasty, these spicy chicken lettuce wraps are best served with cilantro, mint, Thai basil, lime wedges, and crunchy garlic-chile sauce. Everyone grabs a lettuce leaf, places a bit of chicken in the center, and customizes away. Serve the wraps with rice for a complete meal.

 Serves 4

PREP TIME:
10 minutes

COOK TIME:
15 minutes

2 tablespoons soy sauce

1½ teaspoons light brown sugar, packed

2 tablespoons freshly squeezed lime juice

1 teaspoon fish sauce

1½ teaspoons sriracha or sambal oelek

2 tablespoons vegetable oil

3 scallions, white and green parts, sliced

1 lemongrass stalk, bottom third only with tough layers removed, sliced thin

1 to 2 Thai red chiles or other chiles, sliced thin

2 large garlic cloves, minced

1 pound ground chicken or turkey

½ teaspoon kosher salt

1 head Bibb lettuce

1. In a small bowl, whisk the soy sauce, brown sugar, lime juice, fish sauce, and sriracha. Reserve.

2. In a large skillet over medium heat, heat the oil until shimmering. Add the scallions, lemongrass, chiles, and garlic and cook, stirring occasionally, until softened and lightly browned, about 5 minutes.

3. Add the chicken and salt. Cook through, breaking up the meat and tossing occasionally, 5 to 7 minutes.

4. Add the soy sauce mixture and continue cooking, tossing occasionally, until the liquid is almost completely absorbed, 2 to 3 minutes.

5. Serve the chicken mixture with lettuce and the condiments of your choice.

PREP TIP: The chicken can be prepared and kept in the refrigerator 2 days in advance. When you're ready to eat, warm it up in the microwave and serve with crisp lettuce leaves.

Panfried Nashville Hot Chicken Thighs

This fiery, iconic Nashville dish features brined chicken that's double-dredged, fried, and slathered with spicy oil. As is the custom, serve it on top of sliced white bread alongside dill pickle slices. It makes a great sandwich topped with coleslaw, too.

Serves 6

PREP TIME:
15 minutes,
plus overnight
to brine

COOK TIME:
30 minutes

FOR THE CHICKEN

6 boneless, skin-on chicken thighs
1 tablespoon, plus 1 teaspoon kosher salt, divided
1 teaspoon freshly ground black pepper
2 teaspoons white sugar
¼ cup pickle brine, divided
3½ tablespoons Louisiana-style hot sauce, divided

1 cup buttermilk
2 large eggs
2 cups all-purpose flour
1 cup vegetable oil, plus more as needed
6 slices white sandwich bread
1 cup sliced dill pickles

FOR THE SPICY SAUCE

3 tablespoons cayenne pepper
½ teaspoon paprika
½ teaspoon ground cumin
½ teaspoon garlic powder

2 tablespoons unsalted butter
1 tablespoon light brown sugar, packed

TO PREPARE THE CHICKEN

1. Put the chicken in a large, resealable bag. Add the salt, pepper, sugar, pickle brine, and 2 tablespoons of the hot sauce. Tightly seal the bag and squish around the contents to combine. Transfer the bag to the refrigerator to brine overnight.

2. Gather two medium, shallow bowls. In the first, mix the buttermilk, eggs, and 1½ tablespoons of the hot sauce. In the second bowl, combine the flour and salt.

3. Remove the chicken from the refrigerator. Drain and discard the brine and pat the chicken dry with paper towels. Dip the chicken in the buttermilk mixture, followed by the flour mixture, shaking off any excess after each step. Dredge in the flour mixture a second time.

TO COOK THE CHICKEN

4. Fill a cast-iron skillet about ⅓ of the way with vegetable oil. Heat the oil to 350°F over medium-high heat. Carefully place the chicken into the hot oil, breast-side down. Using a candy thermometer or instant-read thermometer, maintain an oil temperature of at least 325°F, adjusting the heat as needed, fry until an instant-read thermometer inserted into the thickest part of the chicken reads 165°F, 8 to 10 minutes per side. Reserve ⅓ cup of the frying oil.

5. Transfer the chicken to a rack to drain.

TO MAKE THE SPICY SAUCE

6. In a small saucepan over medium heat, combine the cayenne pepper, paprika, cumin, and garlic powder and toast until fragrant, 1 to 2 minutes. Add the butter, served frying oil, and brown sugar, whisking to combine. Reduce the heat to low and simmer for 10 minutes.

7. Brush the chicken pieces with the sauce on both sides. Serve the chicken on white bread, with pickles and extra sauce.

Chicken Vesuvio

FREEZER-FRIENDLY · MAKE AHEAD · ONE POT

The origins of chicken Vesuvio—a lemony, garlicky dish served at Chicago's classic Italian restaurants and steakhouses—are up for debate, but the dish gets its name from the volcano most famous for destroying the city of Pompeii in 79 CE. Try giving steak or pork chops the same treatment as this chicken.

Serves 4 to 6

PREP TIME:
15 minutes

COOK TIME:
1 hour
25 minutes

3 tablespoons extra-virgin olive oil
6 bone-in, skin-on chicken thighs
Kosher salt
Freshly ground black pepper
4 large russet potatoes, cut into wedges
8 large garlic cloves, minced

1 cup dry white wine, such as pinot grigio
1 cup low-sodium chicken broth
1½ teaspoons dried oregano
1 teaspoon dried rosemary
1 teaspoon dried thyme
¼ teaspoon ground nutmeg
1 cup frozen peas, thawed
2 tablespoons unsalted butter

1. Adjust the oven rack to the lower-middle position and preheat the oven to 450°F.

2. In a large Dutch oven over high heat on the stovetop, heat the oil.

3. Season the chicken all over with salt and pepper. Working in 2 batches, if necessary, cook the chicken in the Dutch oven until it is a golden brown on all sides, about 10 minutes. Transfer to a platter.

4. Reduce the heat to medium-high. Add the potatoes to the Dutch oven and cook until they are golden brown, stirring occasionally, about 10 minutes.

5. Reduce the heat to medium. Add the garlic and sauté for 1 minute, then add the white wine. Stir to scrape up any brown bits on the bottom of the Dutch oven. Add the broth, oregano, rosemary, thyme, and nutmeg.

6. Return the chicken to the pan over medium-high heat. Stir to combine and bring the mixture to a boil.

7. Transfer the Dutch oven to the oven to bake until the potatoes are fork-tender and the chicken is cooked through, and an instant-read thermometer inserted into the center registers 165°F, about 35 minutes. Add the peas to the pan during the last 5 minutes of cooking and stir to combine.

8. Transfer the chicken and potatoes to a platter. Place the Dutch oven on the stovetop over medium heat and the swirl the butter into the sauce. When the butter is melted and the sauce is slightly thickened, pour it over the chicken and potatoes and serve.

Pan-Seared Chicken Saltimbocca

MAKE AHEAD · ONE POT

Topped with prosciutto and threaded with fresh, piney sage, pan-seared chicken saltimbocca is finished with a lemon-laced white wine sauce. Serve it with a lightly dressed green salad for contrast and crunch.

PREP TIME:
15 minutes

COOK TIME:
20 minutes

4 (4-ounce) boneless, skinless chicken breasts
Kosher salt
Freshly ground black pepper
4 thin slices prosciutto
8 large sage leaves
½ cup all-purpose flour
2 tablespoons extra-virgin olive oil

4 tablespoons unsalted butter, sliced into tablespoons, divided
¼ cup dry white wine
1 cup low-sodium chicken broth
1 tablespoon freshly squeezed lemon juice
2 tablespoons minced fresh flat-leaf parsley

1. Place each chicken breast between two pieces of plastic wrap and, using a meat mallet or rolling pin, pound to a ¼-inch thickness. Season with salt and pepper.

2. Top each piece of chicken with a slice of prosciutto, trimming it to fit and pressing it so it adheres to the meat. Place 2 sage leaves on top of each breast, securing them in place vertically with a toothpick. Dust each breast with flour, shaking off any excess.

3. In a large skillet over medium-high heat, heat the oil and 2 tablespoons of the butter until melted. Working in batches of two, place the breasts in the skillet, prosciutto-side up. Sear for 4 minutes. Flip the chicken and cook just until the prosciutto starts to shrink, about 1 minute more. Transfer to a plate, repeating the process with the remaining chicken. Discard any fat and wipe out the skillet.

4. Add the wine and cook until the liquid is reduced by half, about 2 minutes. Add the broth and lemon juice and cook until reduced by half again, about 3 minutes more.

5. Add the remaining 2 tablespoons of butter to the skillet. Reduce the heat to medium. Return the chicken to the skillet, prosciutto-side up. Simmer until cooked through, about 2 minutes. Serve topped with the pan sauce and parsley.

Tex-Mex Chicken and Cheese Enchiladas Verde

FREEZER-FRIENDLY · MAKE AHEAD

Although this enchilada recipe calls for a can of prepared sauce, I recommend souping up the canned stuff with cumin, ground chili powder, and a pinch of unsweetened cocoa. Feel free to riff as you see fit.

Serves 4

PREP TIME:
20 minutes

COOK TIME:
55 minutes,
plus
10 minutes
to rest

2½ pounds boneless, skinless chicken thighs
1 (32-ounce) container of chicken broth
2 dried bay leaves
2 fresh thyme sprigs
1 teaspoon dried oregano
1 onion, quartered
½ teaspoon black peppercorns, whole

Nonstick cooking spray
1 (32-ounce) can green enchilada sauce
3 cups Chihuahua or Monterey Jack cheese
8 taco-sized flour tortillas, warmed
1 cup sour cream, for serving

1. In a medium saucepan over medium heat, heat the chicken, broth, bay leaves, thyme sprigs, oregano, onion, and peppercorns. Bring to a boil and simmer until the chicken is cooked through and is no longer pink, about 15 to 20 minutes.

2. Remove the chicken from liquid. Discard the liquid or save it for another use. Using two forks or your hands, shred the meat, discarding any fatty or tough parts.

3. Adjust the oven rack to the lower-middle position and preheat the oven to 375°F. Spray a 9-by-13-inch baking sheet with nonstick cooking spray. Spread ¼ cup of the enchilada sauce on the bottom of the pan.

4. Working one at a time, place about ¼ cup of the chicken and ¼ cup of the cheese along the center of each tortilla. Roll each tortilla over the filling and place seam-side down in the prepared baking sheet. Repeat the process until the filling is gone, tightly packing the enchiladas side by side in a row. Spoon the remaining sauce evenly over the enchiladas. Top with the remaining cheese and transfer to the oven to bake until the cheese is brown and bubbly, about 35 minutes.

5. Remove from the oven and let rest for 10 minutes. Serve with the sour cream.

PREP TIP: The enchiladas can be prepared and assembled up to a day in advance. Store the pan, covered, in the refrigerator. When you're ready to cook it, remove from the refrigerator 15 minutes in advance and add an additional 10 to 15 minutes of cooking time.

Thyme and Cider Vinegar Turkey Breast

When you're hankering for Thanksgiving flavors, this cozy brined turkey offers the perfect fix. It comes together in no time and requires minimal attention while it roasts. However, the results are certainly impressive.

Serves 6

PREP TIME:
10 minutes,
plus overnight
to brine

COOK TIME:
1 hour
35 minutes,
plus
10 minutes
to rest

1 (3-pound) turkey
   breast, boneless
6 cups apple cider vinegar
⅓ cup light brown sugar, packed
½ cup, plus ½ teaspoon
   kosher salt, divided
1 tablespoon black
   peppercorns,
   coarsely crushed
1 medium orange, sliced
8 garlic cloves, crushed

3 fresh thyme sprigs
3 dried bay leaves
½ teaspoon freshly
   ground black pepper
2 tablespoons extra-virgin
   olive oil
1 cup water, plus more
   as needed
2 teaspoons cornstarch
¼ cup water

1. Place the turkey in a 2½-gallon resealable bag or a container large enough to hold it. Add the apple cider vinegar, brown sugar, ½ cup of the salt, the peppercorns, orange slices, garlic, thyme sprigs, and bay leaves. Seal the bag, squish the contents around to combine, and transfer to the refrigerator to brine overnight.

2. Adjust the oven rack to the lower-middle position and preheat the oven to 325°F.

3. Remove the turkey from the brine and discard the liquid. Pat the turkey dry using paper towels.

4. Put the turkey on a rack in a roasting pan. Rub the skin with ground pepper, the remaining ½ teaspoon of the salt, and the oil. Transfer to the oven to cook for 1 hour. Then, baste, rotate the turkey, and add 1 cup of water to the bottom of the roasting pan. Continue roasting for about 30 more minutes, or until an instant-read thermometer inserted into the thickest part reads 165°F.

5. Transfer the turkey to a cutting board to rest, loosely tented with foil, for 10 minutes.

6. Skim the fat from the pan and place it over medium heat. Mix the cornstarch with the water. Whisk the cornstarch mixture into the sauce and simmer until the gravy is thickened, about 2 minutes. Carve the turkey and serve with the gravy.

PREPARATION TIP: If the turkey starts to look too dark while cooking, loosely tent it with foil and continue cooking. Remove the foil and let the skin crisp up during the last 15 minutes of cooking.

Grilled Jerk Turkey Legs

FREEZER-FRIENDLY · MAKE AHEAD · ONE POT

Hot and fragrant, spiced jerk chicken is a famous Jamaican dish. A style of cooking that originated from those living on islands throughout the Caribbean Sea, jerk meats are marinated in spices and typically cooked over a wood fire. Here, turkey legs stand in for chicken, offering an update on the iconic mainstay.

Serves 6

PREP TIME:
15 minutes,
plus overnight
to marinate

COOK TIME:
1 hour, plus
10 minutes
to rest

FOR THE JERK SAUCE

2 teaspoons ground allspice

½ teaspoon ground cinnamon

½ teaspoon ground nutmeg

1 teaspoon kosher salt

1 teaspoon freshly ground
black pepper

½ teaspoon fresh thyme leaves

¼ cup light brown sugar, packed

2 tablespoons soy sauce

¼ cup freshly squeezed
lime juice

1 tablespoon apple
cider vinegar

½ cup peanut oil or vegetable oil

3 scallions, coarsely chopped

8 medium garlic cloves

2 tablespoons minced ginger

2 habanero or Scotch
bonnet chiles, seeded,
membranes removed

FOR THE TURKEY

6 turkey drumsticks (about
4½ pounds total)

2 tablespoons rum, such
as Bacardi Gold

Nonstick cooking
spray (optional)

TO MAKE THE JERK SAUCE

1. Add the allspice, cinnamon, nutmeg, salt, pepper, thyme, brown sugar, soy sauce, lime juice, apple cider vinegar, and oil to a blender. Puree. Add the scallions, garlic, ginger, and chiles and puree until smooth. Place half of the sauce in an airtight container and transfer to the refrigerator.

TO MAKE THE TURKEY

2. In a resealable plastic bag, put the turkey, rum, and the unrefrigerated half of the jerk sauce. Seal the bag and squish the contents around to distribute the sauce. Transfer to the refrigerator to marinate overnight or for up to 2 days.

3. Light a charcoal grill or heat a gas grill to medium-high heat (375°F). Alternatively, spray a grill pan with nonstick cooking spray and heat it on medium-high heat on the stovetop. Drain and discard the marinade and pat the turkey dry with paper towels. Place ¼ cup of the reserved jerk sauce in a small bowl to use for basting. Reserve the remainder for serving.

4. Once the grill is hot, clean and oil the grill grate. Place the turkey on the grill. Grill until the skin is crisp and charred, about 4 minutes per quarter turn. Move the meat to a cooler part of the grill and continue cooking over indirect heat, turning and basting occasionally with sauce until a glistening crust forms and an instant-read thermometer registers 165°F when inserted into the thickest part of the leg, about 35 to 45 minutes.

5. Remove from the grill, transfer to a platter, and let rest 10 minutes. Serve with the remaining jerk sauce.

PREP TIP: If you have a gas grill, turn one burner off and leave the remaining burners lit to maintain medium heat.

Bacon-Wrapped Roasted Turkey

MAKE AHEAD · ONE POT

This whole roasted turkey uses crumbled bacon butter as the glue that holds a bacon lattice crust in place. But why save it for a holiday? This showy but simple bird is delightful in winter, spring, summer, and fall.

Serves 10 to 12

PREP TIME:
15 minutes

COOK TIME:
4 hours, plus
20 minutes
to rest

8 tablespoons unsalted butter
1 tablespoon dried sage
1 tablespoon dried thyme
2 tablespoons garlic powder

2 (12-ounce) packages hardwood-smoked bacon, divided
1 (12- to 15-pound) whole turkey
2 cups water

1. In a food processor, pulse the butter, sage, thyme, garlic powder, and 4 slices of the bacon until smooth.

2. Adjust the oven rack to the lower-third position and preheat the oven to 325°F. Remove the giblets and neck from the turkey's cavity and discard or save (see page 127).

3. Place the turkey on a metal rack in a large roasting pan. Rub the bird all over with the butter mixture. Wrap each leg with 2 slices of bacon and each wing with 1 slice of bacon, tucking the ends into the crease between the leg and the breast. On a large sheet of parchment paper, weave a "blanket" of bacon using eight slices in each direction, much like you would weave dough on the top of a lattice pie. With the bacon still on the parchment paper, carefully flip it to top the bird. Discard the wax paper and tuck the bacon under the bird and into its creases.

4. Pour the water into the bottom of the roasting pan. Transfer the turkey to the oven to bake, basting every 45 minutes with juices in the roasting pan, until the meat is no longer pink at the bone and its juices run clear, 3½ to 4 hours, and when an instant-read thermometer inserted into the thigh and between the thigh and breast reads 165°F.

5. Remove the turkey from the oven and transfer it to a cutting board to rest for 15 to 20 minutes before carving. Serve.

> **INGREDIENT TIP:** Buy the longest strips of bacon you can find, as they'll provide the best coverage for your turkey. You want to avoid buying center-cut bacon for this dish, as it tends to be too short.

Juicy Grilled Turkey Burgers

Dry, lifeless turkey burgers are enough to turn anyone off of having them again. Try a good one, though, and you'll be hooked. Consider this your starting point, but feel free to customize it by adding your own favorite herbs.

Serves 6

PREP TIME:
10 minutes

COOK TIME:
15 minutes

Nonstick cooking spray (optional)

1¼ pounds ground turkey

1 large egg, lightly beaten

½ cup plain bread crumbs

¼ cup finely chopped onions

1 teaspoon Worcestershire sauce

2 teaspoons Dijon mustard

½ teaspoon kosher salt

½ teaspoon freshly ground black pepper

6 hamburger buns

1. Light a charcoal grill or heat a gas grill to medium-high heat (375°F). Alternatively, spray a grill pan with nonstick cooking spray and heat on medium-high heat on the stovetop.

2. In a large bowl, mix the turkey, egg, bread crumbs, onions, Worcestershire sauce, mustard, salt, and pepper until just combined. Do not over-mix.

3. Once the grill is hot, grease the grates and place the burgers on the grill over indirect heat. Cook for 6 to 7 minutes on each side, or until an instant-read thermometer inserted into the center reads 165°F and the juices run clear. Serve on buns with the condiments of your choice.

MEASUREMENT CONVERSIONS

VOLUME EQUIVALENTS	U.S. STANDARD	U.S. STANDARD (OUNCES)	METRIC (APPROXIMATE)
LIQUID	2 tablespoons	1 fl. oz.	30 mL
	¼ cup	2 fl. oz.	60 mL
	½ cup	4 fl. oz.	120 mL
	1 cup	8 fl. oz.	240 mL
	1½ cups	12 fl. oz.	355 mL
	2 cups or 1 pint	16 fl. oz.	475 mL
	4 cups or 1 quart	32 fl. oz.	1 L
	1 gallon	128 fl. oz.	4 L
DRY	⅛ teaspoon	–	0.5 mL
	¼ teaspoon	–	1 mL
	½ teaspoon	–	2 mL
	¾ teaspoon	–	4 mL
	1 teaspoon	–	5 mL
	1 tablespoon	–	15 mL
	¼ cup	–	59 mL
	⅓ cup	–	79 mL
	½ cup	–	118 mL
	⅔ cup	–	156 mL
	¾ cup	–	177 mL
	1 cup	–	235 mL
	2 cups or 1 pint	–	475 mL
	3 cups	–	700 mL
	4 cups or 1 quart	–	1 L
	½ gallon	–	2 L
	1 gallon	–	4 L

OVEN TEMPERATURES

FAHRENHEIT	CELSIUS (APPROXIMATE)
250°F	120°C
300°F	150°C
325°F	165°C
350°F	180°C
375°F	190°C
400°F	200°C
425°F	220°C
450°F	230°C

WEIGHT EQUIVALENTS

U.S. STANDARD	METRIC (APPROXIMATE)
½ ounce	15 g
1 ounce	30 g
2 ounces	60 g
4 ounces	115 g
8 ounces	225 g
12 ounces	340 g
16 ounces or 1 pound	455 g

RESOURCES

Sharon Tyler Herbst and Rob Herbst's *The New Food Lover's Companion* (Barron's Educational Series, 5th edition, 2013) is an enlarged, enhanced reference written for discerning home chefs and anyone who wants to beef up their food know-how.

National Geographic's Food Education collection, NationalGeographic.org /education/food-education, offers a fascinating look at food history, culture, and topical information on food issues.

David Joachim's authoritative, encyclopedia-style *The Food Substitutions Bible* (Robert Rose, 2nd edition, September 2, 2010) is a wonderfully helpful book with over 6,500 recommendations for ingredient, equipment, and technique substitutions that you can swap out in a pinch, eliminating the need for extra trips to the store.

Up your cooking game with TheChefAndTheDish.com, a kitchen-to-kitchen culinary experience where chefs from the world over teach private, one-on-one Skype-based classes to fledgling and expert-level home cooks alike.

Instructables.com/cooking is a free, community-based site with photo tutorials that'll help you set up your own kitchen and gain cooking confidence with low commitment. Sign up for a lesson series on meat to learn about products and techniques you can apply to any recipe.

MasterClass.com, features a roundup of video tutorials. It also curates single-class instruction from icons in the field, such as the chefs Thomas Keller, Gordon Ramsay, and Alice Waters, as well as *Wine Spectator*'s James Suckling. Monthly memberships and single-class sign-ups are available.

INDEX

ACKNOWLEDGMENTS

I'd like to thank Mike, Hayden, and Anders, who supported and encouraged me along this journey in the midst of a global pandemic. I also extend a loving thank-you to my sister, Katie, and mom, Elizabeth, for their encouraging words and inspiration. Finally, I want to thank my publisher, Callisto Media, for this amazing opportunity, and my editor, Marjorie DeWitt, for her insight and keen eye for details.

ABOUT THE AUTHOR

 **JENNIFER OLVERA** is a food writer, recipe developer, and author of *Easy Mexican Food Favorites, The Meat Lovers' Slow Cooker Cookbook, Food Lovers' Guide to Chicago, Chicago Select,* and the *United Polaris* cookbook, a partnership with United Airlines' Polaris lounge and chefs from Charlie Trotter's not-for-profit, The Trotter Project. A former columnist for *Serious Eats* and dining critic for *Chicago* magazine, she also contributed to *The Chicago Food Encyclopedia,* Zagat Survey's printed guides and blog, and the food and travel sections of the *Chicago Tribune,* the *Chicago Sun-Times,* and the *Los Angeles Times.* This is her seventh book and fourth cookbook.

CPSIA information can be obtained
at www.ICGtesting.com
Printed in the USA
JSHW020902091120
9335JS00001B/1